Word ∞ master

KB019074

3 in 1 본책 + 미니북 + 워크북 구성의

완벽한 영단어 학습 시스템

+

한 번 더 업그레이드!

업그레이드 방법은 뒷면에 >>

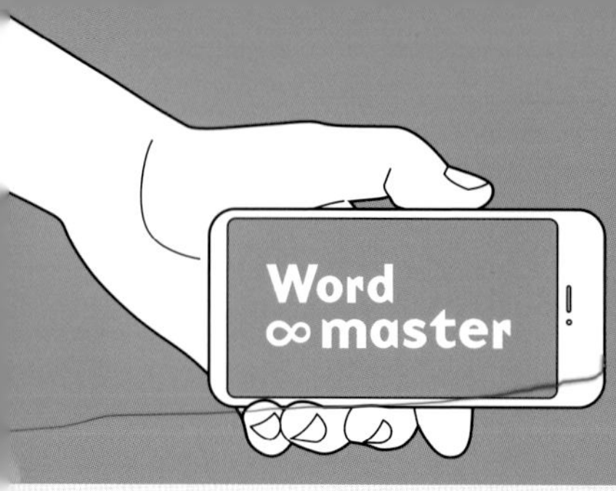

OFF LINE 도서 에 ON LINE 학습앱 을 더해

업그레이드

워드마스터 학습앱 How To Use

Step. 1 앱 설치 및 회원가입

» 앱 바로가기

Step. 2 마이룸에서 학습앱 코드 입력

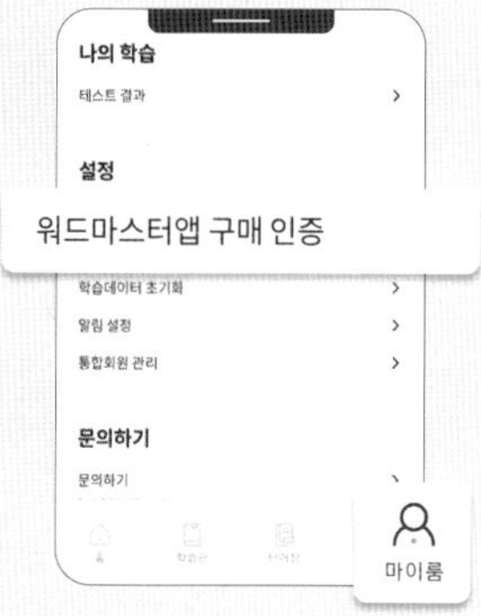

Step. 3 학습관에서 데이터 다운로드

Step. 4 학습관에서 단어/음성 암기부터 TEST까지

Step. 5 단어장에서 헷갈리는 단어 복습

Step. 6 마이룸에서 누적 테스트 결과로 학습 상태 점검

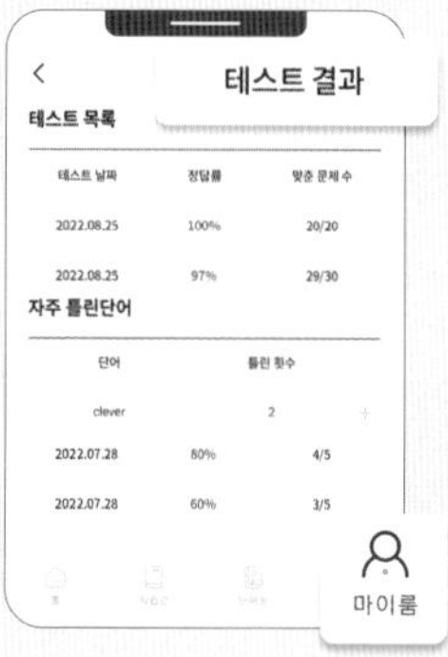

학습앱 코드 UUDEQMWXS

※ 코드는 1회 등록 가능합니다.

Word ∞ master

고등 BASIC

Workbook

Word
∞ master

고등
BASIC

DAILY CHECK-UP

A 다음 영어 단어에 해당하는 우리말 뜻을 쓰시오.

01 include ______
02 refuse ______
03 carry out ______
04 provide ______
05 similar ______
06 disappear ______
07 increase ______
08 superior ______
09 belief ______
10 supply ______
11 moment ______
12 reject ______
13 improve ______
14 inferior ______
15 emerge ______
16 produce ______
17 practical ______
18 fade ______
19 share ______
20 grief ______

B 다음 우리말 뜻에 해당하는 영어 단어를 쓰시오.

01 무관심한 ______
02 흔한, 보통의 ______
03 감정, 정서 ______
04 진보한, 상급의 ______
05 회복하다, 복구되다 ______
06 찾다, 추구하다 ______
07 ~와 우연히 만나다 ______
08 경험하다, 경험 ______
09 목적, 목표로 하다 ______
10 고려하다, ~으로 여기다 ______
11 성공, 성공작 ______
12 ~에 의존[의지]하다 ______
13 확실한, 어떤 ______
14 감소하다, 감소시키다 ______
15 약간의, 하찮은 ______
16 양, 수량 ______
17 상황, 위치 ______
18 실패, 실패작, 고장 ______
19 표현하다, 급행의 ______
20 받아들이다, 수락하다 ______

C 다음 영어 단어의 유의어 또는 반의어를 쓰시오.

01 improve	=	________	06 emotion	=	________
02 quantity	=	________	07 common	↔	________
03 seek	=	________	08 include	↔	________
04 superior	↔	________	09 situation	=	________
05 refuse	↔	________	10 carry out	=	________

D 다음 문장의 빈칸에 주어진 철자로 시작하는 알맞은 단어를 쓰시오.

01 Two months later, another computer company tried a s________ experiment.
2개월 후에 또 다른 컴퓨터 회사가 비슷한 실험을 시도했다.

02 Recently, the rate of youth unemployment has suddenly i________.
최근에 청년 실업률이 갑자기 증가했다.

03 More a________ greenbeam laser pointers came to be introduced.
더 발전된 초록빛 레이저 포인터가 도입되었다.

04 They looked cold and i________ to the suffering of the victims.
그들은 희생자들의 고통에 냉정하고 무관심해 보였다.

05 The sound of my footsteps f________ away into the emptiness of the streets.
내 발자국 소리는 거리의 공허함 속으로 사라졌다.

06 The executive always came up with p________ ideas at the conference table.
그 간부는 회의 석상에서 항상 실용적인 아이디어를 생각해 냈다.

DAY 02

A 다음 영어 단어에 해당하는 우리말 뜻을 쓰시오.

01 found ____________

02 achieve ____________

03 expose ____________

04 reliable ____________

05 unite ____________

06 rapid ____________

07 vital ____________

08 accomplish ____________

09 overcome ____________

10 crime ____________

11 illegal ____________

12 organ ____________

13 separate ____________

14 lead to ____________

15 establish ____________

16 deserve ____________

17 period ____________

18 reveal ____________

19 mislead ____________

20 combine ____________

B 다음 우리말 뜻에 해당하는 영어 단어를 쓰시오.

01 ~와 잘 지내다 ____________

02 인식하다, 인정하다 ____________

03 쫓다, 추적하다, 추적 ____________

04 양, 총계가 ~이 되다 ____________

05 연결하다, 관련시키다 ____________

06 ~을 처리하다 ____________

07 숨기다, 비밀로 하다 ____________

08 과정, 처리[가공]하다 ____________

09 바치다, 전념하다 ____________

10 인지하다, ~으로 여기다 ____________

11 계속하다, 연장하다 ____________

12 지역의, 현지의 ____________

13 무작위의, 임의의 ____________

14 역사적인, 역사(상)의 ____________

15 전문가, 숙련된 ____________

16 바치다, 헌신하다 ____________

17 완료하다, 완전한 ____________

18 지친, 고갈된 ____________

19 10년, 10년간 ____________

20 자선 단체, 자비심 ____________

C 다음 영어 단어의 유의어 또는 반의어를 쓰시오.

01 amount ⊜ __________

02 perceive ⊜ __________

03 continue ↔ __________

04 exhausted ⊜ __________

05 reveal ↔ __________

06 combine ↔ __________

07 achieve ⊜ __________

08 vital ⊜ __________

09 lead to ⊜ __________

10 random ↔ __________

D 다음 문장의 빈칸에 주어진 철자로 시작하는 알맞은 단어를 쓰시오.

01 Maps still carry an aura of being r__________ and bias-free.
지도는 믿을 수 있으며 편견이 없다는 느낌을 여전히 지니고 있다.

02 You worked hard to enter that college, and you d__________ your success.
당신은 그 대학에 들어가기 위해 열심히 공부했으니 마땅히 성공할 만하다.

03 Countries with more r__________ economic growth do not experience a greater increase in happiness.
더 빠른 경제 성장을 보이는 나라들의 행복이 더 크게 증가하지는 않는다.

04 The spectators d__________ time and money to watch a game in person.
관중은 직접 경기를 보기 위해 시간과 돈을 바친다.

05 A quarter of the surface area is e__________ to the atmosphere.
표면적의 4분의 1이 대기에 노출된다.

06 We can begin to consciously d__________ __________ the challenge using our reasoning abilities.
우리는 우리의 추론 능력을 사용하여 의식적으로 어려운 문제를 다루기 시작할 수 있다.

DAY 03

A 다음 영어 단어에 해당하는 우리말 뜻을 쓰시오.

01 benefit ______
02 distance ______
03 contain ______
04 medical ______
05 probable ______
06 research ______
07 material ______
08 various ______
09 official ______
10 encourage ______
11 trait ______
12 involve ______
13 concentrate ______
14 income ______
15 mark ______
16 investigate ______
17 due ______
18 profit ______
19 pursue ______
20 negative ______

B 다음 우리말 뜻에 해당하는 영어 단어를 쓰시오.

01 바꾸다, 변경하다 ______
02 ~에 따르면 ______
03 감독하다, 직접적인 ______
04 세부 사항, 상세 ______
05 접촉하다, 연락하다 ______
06 검진하다, 시험하다 ______
07 ~에 참여하다 ______
08 해결, 결심, 결의 ______
09 찾다, 검색하다 ______
10 공연, 성과, 수행 ______
11 다양한, 다른 ______
12 지식, 알고 있음 ______
13 개정하다, 정정하다 ______
14 낙담시키다, 방해하다 ______
15 방해하다, 어지럽히다 ______
16 기회, 가망 ______
17 무시하다 ______
18 피해, 손상을 입히다 ______
19 (대단히) 놀라게 하다 ______
20 ~을 주의 깊게 살피다 ______

C 다음 영어 단어의 유의어 또는 반의어를 쓰시오.

01 benefit ↔ ______________

02 ignore = ______________

03 various = ______________

04 involve ↔ ______________

05 material = ______________

06 participate in = ______________

07 concentrate ↔ ______________

08 negative ↔ ______________

09 trait = ______________

10 income ↔ ______________

D 다음 문장의 빈칸에 주어진 철자로 시작하는 알맞은 단어를 쓰시오.

01 Because Ethan motivated and e__________ them, they became his most passionate fans.
Ethan이 그들에게 동기를 부여하고 용기를 북돋았기 때문에, 그들은 그의 가장 열정적인 팬이 되었다.

02 The flight m__________ the milestone of her flying over four million miles.
그 비행은 그녀가 400만 마일 넘게 비행한 획기적인 사건을 기록했다.

03 Melatonin simply provides the o__________ instruction to commence the event of sleep.
멜라토닌은 단순히 수면이라는 시합을 시작하게 할 공식적인 지시를 제공한다.

04 Magicians a__________ audiences with seemingly impossible tricks of magic.
마술사들은 외견상 불가능한 마술 기교로 관객들을 놀라게 한다.

05 The dishes c__________ some of the most common foods in the world.
그 요리들은 세계에서 가장 평범한 음식들 중 몇 가지를 포함한다.

06 Children reveal and i__________ mathematical concepts through their own activities or experiences.
아이들은 자기들만의 활동이나 경험을 통해 수학적 개념을 밝히고 조사한다.

DAY 04

A 다음 영어 단어에 해당하는 우리말 뜻을 쓰시오.

01 circumstance ____________
02 development ____________
03 influence ____________
04 occur ____________
05 forecast ____________
06 passion ____________
07 entire ____________
08 emphasize ____________
09 permit ____________
10 immediate ____________
11 environment ____________
12 participation ____________
13 maintain ____________
14 conservative ____________
15 forbid ____________
16 impact ____________
17 emission ____________
18 measure ____________
19 predict ____________
20 respect ____________

B 다음 우리말 뜻에 해당하는 영어 단어를 쓰시오.

01 막다, 예방하다 ____________
02 지지하다, 후원 ____________
03 노력, 수고, 결과 ____________
04 진보하다, 전진하다 ____________
05 ~ 때문에 ____________
06 관점, 시각, 원근법 ____________
07 필요(성), 필수품 ____________
08 경향, 추세, 성향 ____________
09 선호(도) ____________
10 염려, 관련되다 ____________
11 ~을 인식하다, ~을 알다 ____________
12 중요한, 상당한 ____________
13 활동적인, 적극적인 ____________
14 지역 사회, 공동체 ____________
15 A에게 B를 제공하다 ____________
16 규칙적인, 보통의 ____________
17 고대의, 옛날의 ____________
18 결정하다, 밝혀내다 ____________
19 군대, 군대의 ____________
20 기능, 행사, 작용하다 ____________

C 다음 영어 단어의 유의어 또는 반의어를 쓰시오.

01 passion	= ______	06 impact	= ______
02 entire	↔ ______	07 regular	↔ ______
03 environment	= ______	08 maintain	= ______
04 forbid	= ______	09 ancient	↔ ______
05 active	↔ ______	10 immediate	= ______

D 다음 문장의 빈칸에 주어진 철자로 시작하는 알맞은 단어를 쓰시오.

01 Citizens have revealed a p________ for a stable national population.
시민들은 안정적인 국가 인구에 대한 선호를 드러냈다.

02 A s________ aspect of a plant's environment is the presence of other organisms.
식물 환경의 중요한 측면은 다른 생물들의 존재이다.

03 Our senses p________ us ________ a qualitative indication of temperature.
우리의 감각은 우리에게 온도의 정성적인 지표를 제공한다.

04 It has always been our c________ to promote quality health of the students in our school.
우리 학교 학생들의 양질의 건강을 장려하는 것은 항상 우리의 관심사였다.

05 The f________ to drive straight in and out of your garage was very impressive to us.
당신의 차고로 곧장 운전해서 들어가고 나오는 기능은 우리에게 매우 인상적이었다.

06 One message e________ the opportunity to do good.
하나의 메시지는 좋은 일을 할 기회를 강조했다.

DAY 05

A 다음 영어 단어에 해당하는 우리말 뜻을 쓰시오.

01 claim ______________
02 suppose ______________
03 approach ______________
04 refer to ______________
05 gather ______________
06 organize ______________
07 exist ______________
08 arrange ______________
09 crucial ______________
10 aspect ______________
11 purpose ______________
12 describe ______________
13 motivate ______________
14 confuse ______________
15 represent ______________
16 exhibit ______________
17 attract ______________
18 adjust ______________
19 treatment ______________
20 display ______________

B 다음 우리말 뜻에 해당하는 영어 단어를 쓰시오.

01 구입하다, 구입 ______________
02 낙담시키다 ______________
03 사고, 재난, 우연 ______________
04 요구하다, 수요 ______________
05 일반적인, 장군 ______________
06 경보, 불안하게 하다 ______________
07 수수료, 요금 ______________
08 구체적인, 특정한 ______________
09 사례금, 보상하다 ______________
10 ~을 떠맡다 ______________
11 의사소통을 하다 ______________
12 비교하다, 비유하다 ______________
13 무질서, 혼란, 장애 ______________
14 관리하다, 용케 해내다 ______________
15 처리하다, 손잡이 ______________
16 보편적인, 우주의 ______________
17 ~에 주목하다 ______________
18 사과하다 ______________
19 관찰하다, 준수하다 ______________
20 권하다, 추천하다 ______________

C 다음 영어 단어의 유의어 또는 반의어를 쓰시오.

01 disorder = ______________

02 suppose = ______________

03 organize = ______________

04 disappoint ↔ ______________

05 describe = ______________

06 motivate ↔ ______________

07 handle = ______________

08 take on = ______________

09 demand ↔ ______________

10 crucial = ______________

D 다음 문장의 빈칸에 주어진 철자로 시작하는 알맞은 단어를 쓰시오.

01 These are strongly linked to problems of crime and social d__________.
이것들은 범죄와 사회 무질서의 문제들과 강하게 연결되어 있다.

02 As size changed, so did other a__________ of the horses' anatomy.
크기가 바뀌면서, 말의 해부학적 구조의 다른 측면들도 역시 바뀌었다.

03 You can easily forget that you are trying to c__________ with a specific person.
여러분은 자신이 특정한 사람과 의사소통하려 한다는 것을 쉽게 잊어버릴 수 있다.

04 They are temporary activities that can a__________ large numbers of outsiders to a locality.
그것들은 많은 외부인들을 한 지역으로 끌어들일 수 있는 일시적 활동들이다.

05 The hospital is proud to e__________ a collection of paintings by many famous artists.
그 병원은 많은 유명한 화가들의 그림 소장품을 전시하는 것을 자랑스럽게 여긴다.

06 These signs communicate something s__________ about your baby's emotional state.
이러한 신호들은 여러분의 아기의 정서적인 상태에 대한 구체적인 것을 말해 준다.

DAY 06

A 다음 영어 단어에 해당하는 우리말 뜻을 쓰시오.

01 discuss ____________
02 complain ____________
03 appropriate ____________
04 primary ____________
05 category ____________
06 welfare ____________
07 struggle ____________
08 proper ____________
09 poison ____________
10 locate ____________
11 respond ____________
12 invention ____________
13 debate ____________
14 except ____________
15 concept ____________
16 conclude ____________
17 norm ____________
18 indicate ____________
19 replace ____________
20 essential ____________

B 다음 우리말 뜻에 해당하는 영어 단어를 쓰시오.

01 시도, 재판 ____________
02 유일한, 독특한 ____________
03 ~할 여유가 있다 ____________
04 광고하다, 알리다 ____________
05 현실적인, 사실주의의 ____________
06 보충하다, 보충(물) ____________
07 화학의, 화학 물질 ____________
08 판단, 판결, 의견 ____________
09 신용, 학점, 신용하다 ____________
10 제거[배제]하다 ____________
11 표준, 일반적인, 표준의 ____________
12 효율적인, 유능한 ____________
13 이상적인, 이상 ____________
14 유아, 젖먹이 ____________
15 의견, 견해 ____________
16 소비[소모]하다 ____________
17 ~을 다 써 버리다 ____________
18 의식, 인식 ____________
19 살아 있는 ____________
20 소중한, 값비싼 ____________

C 다음 영어 단어의 유의어 또는 반의어를 쓰시오.

01 consume	↔	________	06 unique	↔	________
02 norm	=	________	07 primary	=	________
03 efficient	↔	________	08 eliminate	↔	________
04 discuss	=	________	09 concept	=	________
05 struggle	=	________	10 ideal	↔	________

D 다음 문장의 빈칸에 주어진 철자로 시작하는 알맞은 단어를 쓰시오.

01 Susan felt that she was a v__________ human being with something special.
Susan은 자신이 특별한 것을 지닌 소중한 인간이라는 것을 느꼈다.

02 Several bread companies a__________ sliced bread as “the greatest forward step in the baking industry.”
몇몇 빵 회사가 얇게 썬 빵을 ‘제빵계에서의 가장 위대한 진보’라고 광고했다.

03 She went to the nurse’s station to c__________, but no nurse was there.
그녀는 항의하러 간호사실로 갔지만, 그곳에는 간호사가 아무도 없었다.

04 The missing tooth i__________ that we have to replace it.
빠진 치아는 우리가 그것을 대체해야 한다는 것을 나타낸다.

05 The bakery is usually l__________ far from the front door of a supermarket.
제과점은 보통 슈퍼마켓의 정문에서 멀리 떨어진 곳에 위치한다.

06 The study was in danger of r__________ __________ __________ funds.
그 연구는 자금이 바닥날 위험에 처해 있었다.

A 다음 영어 단어에 해당하는 우리말 뜻을 쓰시오.

01 employ	______	11 average	______
02 brilliant	______	12 application	______
03 factor	______	13 publish	______
04 protest	______	14 obstacle	______
05 barrier	______	15 finance	______
06 appoint	______	16 define	______
07 enormous	______	17 element	______
08 hire	______	18 ordinary	______
09 deadly	______	19 reasonable	______
10 invest	______	20 vast	______

B 다음 우리말 뜻에 해당하는 영어 단어를 쓰시오.

01 때, 경우, 행사	______	11 ~의[할] 가치가 있는	______
02 섞다, 어울리다, 혼합(물)	______	12 성(性), 성별	______
03 ~에 익숙해지다	______	13 독립, 자립	______
04 교육, 훈련	______	14 드문, 희박한	______
05 기부[기증]하다	______	15 이전의, 먼저의	______
06 대안, 대체의	______	16 버리다, 포기하다	______
07 단단한, 확고한, 회사	______	17 믿을 수 없는, 놀라운	______
08 관심, 흥미, 이자	______	18 발견하다, 탐지하다	______
09 겉모습, 출현	______	19 ~을 알아내다	______
10 생물의, 유기농의	______	20 아주 작은[적은]	______

C 다음 영어 단어의 유의어 또는 반의어를 쓰시오.

01 incredible = ____________

02 employ = ____________

03 previous ↔ ____________

04 brilliant = ____________

05 deadly = ____________

06 enormous ↔ ____________

07 reasonable = ____________

08 ordinary ↔ ____________

09 appoint = ____________

10 firm = ____________

D 다음 문장의 빈칸에 주어진 철자로 시작하는 알맞은 단어를 쓰시오.

01 Soil contains various amounts of o__________ materials, minerals, and rocks.
토양은 다양한 양의 유기물, 무기물, 그리고 암석을 포함한다.

02 The tornado was, according to weather experts, a very r__________ case in New England.
날씨 전문가들에 따르면, 그 토네이도는 뉴잉글랜드에서는 매우 드문 경우였다.

03 Olivers are an a__________ currency usable only in Bathampton.
Olivers는 Bathampton에서만 사용할 수 있는 대체 통화이다.

04 We d__________ fairness as equal sharing as long as the sharing lies in the future.
우리는 공유가 미래에 존재하는 한 공정을 균등한 공유로 정의한다.

05 Smoke detectors sound an alarm when smoke from a fire is d__________.
화재로부터 연기가 감지되면 연기 감지기가 경보를 울린다.

06 He believed that American i__________ would lead to a new age, free of class and social distinctions.
그는 미국의 독립이 계급 차별과 사회적 차별이 없는 새로운 시대로 이어질 것이라고 믿었다.

DAY 08

A 다음 영어 단어에 해당하는 우리말 뜻을 쓰시오.

01 satisfaction ______________
02 majority ______________
03 comfort ______________
04 ease ______________
05 enable ______________
06 preserve ______________
07 document ______________
08 trend ______________
09 infection ______________
10 grab ______________
11 household ______________
12 insurance ______________
13 economic ______________
14 celebrate ______________
15 sentence ______________
16 accurate ______________
17 escape ______________
18 precise ______________
19 compete ______________
20 rather than ______________

B 다음 우리말 뜻에 해당하는 영어 단어를 쓰시오.

01 상쾌하게 하는 ______________
02 신문, 간행물, 일기 ______________
03 차량, 운송 수단 ______________
04 사적인, 사유의 ______________
05 수술, 운영, 작업 ______________
06 속하다 ______________
07 정반대의, 맞은편의 ______________
08 옮기다, 환승 ______________
09 제출하다, 굴복하다 ______________
10 혁신하다, 쇄신하다 ______________
11 ~의 책임[탓]으로 돌리다 ______________
12 이론, 학설 ______________
13 추정하다, 평가하다 ______________
14 증명하다, 시위하다 ______________
15 재난, 재앙 ______________
16 통찰력, 이해 ______________
17 할당하다, 임명하다 ______________
18 수십의, 많은 ______________
19 피하다, 막다 ______________
20 운동, 움직임, 동작 ______________

C 다음 영어 단어의 유의어 또는 반의어를 쓰시오.

01 comfort	= ________	06 opposite	= ________
02 satisfaction	= ________	07 escape	= ________
03 majority	↔ ________	08 assign	= ________
04 grab	= ________	09 accurate	↔ ________
05 blame	= ________	10 submit	= ________

D 다음 문장의 빈칸에 주어진 철자로 시작하는 알맞은 단어를 쓰시오.

01 You will need to make some e________ of how long you need together.
당신은 얼마나 오랜 시간을 함께 필요로 하는지에 대한 약간의 추정을 해야 할 필요가 있을 것이다.

02 We have lost our ability to i________ and create new products.
우리는 혁신하여 신제품을 만들어 내는 능력을 잃었다.

03 Arranging things will e________ you to avoid costly and dangerous mistakes.
물건을 정리하는 것은 여러분이 대가가 크고 위험한 실수를 피하는 것을 가능하게 할 것이다.

04 The kind of tasks involved are sowing seeds outside and t________ vegetable plants.
포함되는 일의 종류는 밖에서 씨 뿌리기와 채소 식물 옮기기이다.

05 The leader of the town chose a day when James d________ his skills.
그 마을의 지도자는 James가 그의 기술을 증명하는 날을 정했다.

06 We know about dinosaurs because their bones have been p________ as fossils.
그들의 뼈가 화석으로 보존되어 있기 때문에 우리는 공룡에 대해 알고 있다.

DAY 09

A 다음 영어 단어에 해당하는 우리말 뜻을 쓰시오.

01 severe ______
02 guarantee ______
03 violent ______
04 punish ______
05 crisis ______
06 recall ______
07 adequate ______
08 analyze ______
09 delay ______
10 genetic ______
11 comment ______
12 agent ______
13 aggressive ______
14 rotate ______
15 settle ______
16 glow ______
17 genius ______
18 register ______
19 acknowledge ______
20 civilization ______

B 다음 우리말 뜻에 해당하는 영어 단어를 쓰시오.

01 ~에 바탕을 두다 ______
02 저지르다, 전념하다 ______
03 건설하다, 구성하다 ______
04 부담, (짐을) 싣다 ______
05 성숙한, 자라다 ______
06 선언하다, (과세품을) 신고하다 ______
07 제조하다, 생산하다 ______
08 편집하다, 사설 ______
09 밀다, 찌르다 ______
10 A에게 B를 상기시키다 ______
11 장비를 갖추다 ______
12 점차, 서서히 ______
13 기업의, 법인의 ______
14 부인하다, 거부하다 ______
15 경계하는, 알리다 ______
16 지속 가능한 ______
17 행동, 태도 ______
18 무죄인, 순수한 ______
19 유죄의 ______
20 평판, 명성 ______

C 다음 영어 단어의 유의어 또는 반의어를 쓰시오.

01 declare = ______________

02 comment = ______________

03 load = ______________

04 punish ↔ ______________

05 reputation = ______________

06 gradually ↔ ______________

07 glow = ______________

08 construct ↔ ______________

09 adequate = ______________

10 guilty ↔ ______________

D 다음 문장의 빈칸에 주어진 철자로 시작하는 알맞은 단어를 쓰시오.

01 It is difficult to imagine the significance of cats to early c__________.
초기 문명에서 고양이의 중요성을 상상하는 것은 어렵다.

02 Journalists cannot work for the media without being r__________ and obtaining a press card.
기자는 등록되어 기자증을 얻지 않고는 언론을 위해 일할 수 없다.

03 How can you s__________ differences if you don't honestly talk them out?
만약 당신이 솔직하게 차이점들을 털어놓지 않으면, 어떻게 그것들을 해결할 수 있겠는가?

04 Living together in human society often requires restraining a__________ behavior.
인간 사회에서 함께 살아가는 것은 종종 공격적인 행동을 억제하는 것을 필요로 한다.

05 She had nothing to g__________ that she would pay back the loan.
그녀는 대출금을 갚을 것이라고 보증할 것이 아무것도 없었다.

06 Its metabolism shifts as it either prepares to divide or m__________ and differentiates into a specialized cell.
그것은 분열할 준비를 하거나 혹은 성숙하여 특화된 세포로 분화하면서 그것의 물질대사가 변화한다.

DAY 10

A 다음 영어 단어에 해당하는 우리말 뜻을 쓰시오.

01 obvious ______________
02 possess ______________
03 cautious ______________
04 ancestor ______________
05 tremble ______________
06 length ______________
07 permanent ______________
08 apparent ______________
09 victim ______________
10 broaden ______________
11 athlete ______________
12 logical ______________
13 qualified ______________
14 electricity ______________
15 persist ______________
16 departure ______________
17 inherit ______________
18 drag ______________
19 extend ______________
20 contribute to ______________

B 다음 우리말 뜻에 해당하는 영어 단어를 쓰시오.

01 ~와 관계가 있다 ______________
02 수직의, 세로의 ______________
03 주목할 만한 ______________
04 퇴직하다, 철수하다 ______________
05 저항하다, 견디다 ______________
06 일시적인, 임시의 ______________
07 고안하다, 발명하다 ______________
08 제한하다, 한정하다 ______________
09 수평(선)의, 가로의 ______________
10 개혁하다, 개선 ______________
11 제물, 희생하다 ______________
12 개인, 개개의 ______________
13 통제하다, 조절하다 ______________
14 명확히 하다, 정화하다 ______________
15 암기하다, 기억하다 ______________
16 (배 · 항공기 등을) 타고 ______________
17 처음의, 머리글자 ______________
18 수용하다, 포옹하다 ______________
19 섬세한, 연약한, 정교한 ______________
20 구조하다, 구조 ______________

C 다음 영어 단어의 유의어 또는 반의어를 쓰시오.

01 obvious ⊜ ____________

02 temporary ⇔ ____________

03 tremble ⊜ ____________

04 horizontal ⇔ ____________

05 embrace ⇔ ____________

06 broaden ⊜ ____________

07 departure ⇔ ____________

08 regulate ⊜ ____________

09 ancestor ⇔ ____________

10 restrict ⊜ ____________

D 다음 문장의 빈칸에 주어진 철자로 시작하는 알맞은 단어를 쓰시오.

01 Some young children who attend preschool are very c__________.
유치원에 다니는 일부 어린아이들은 매우 조심성 있다.

02 The r__________ growth of art exhibitions can be analysed in this light.
예술 전시회의 주목할 만한 성장은 이러한 관점에서 분석될 수 있다.

03 They made incredible s__________ and overcame all obstacles to complete a project.
그들은 믿을 수 없는 희생을 치렀고 모든 장애를 극복하고 프로젝트를 완성했다.

04 The last thing that she expected was to i__________ such wealth.
그녀가 전혀 예상치 못한 것은 그런 부를 물려받는 것이었다.

05 The i__________ stages of a relationship are usually conflict-free.
관계의 초기 단계는 대개 갈등이 없다.

06 Blue was more d__________ and prettier, thus more proper for girls.
파란색은 더 섬세하고 예뻐서 여자아이들에게 더 적합했다.

DAY 11

A 다음 영어 단어에 해당하는 우리말 뜻을 쓰시오.

01 foster ______
02 population ______
03 ingredient ______
04 scatter ______
05 go through ______
06 split ______
07 multiple ______
08 friction ______
09 nurture ______
10 wound ______
11 cause ______
12 capacity ______
13 trace ______
14 disclose ______
15 ability ______
16 discover ______
17 massive ______
18 negotiate ______
19 conflict ______
20 accuse ______

B 다음 우리말 뜻에 해당하는 영어 단어를 쓰시오.

01 ~하는 데 어려움을 겪다 ______
02 압력, 압박(감) ______
03 선거, 당선 ______
04 결과, 영향(력) ______
05 뛰어난, 현저한 ______
06 ~으로 간주되다 ______
07 철사, (전선을) 연결하다 ______
08 대화, 대담 ______
09 역경, 불운 ______
10 외국의, 이국적인 ______
11 생물학의 ______
12 탄소 ______
13 비유, 유사, 유추 ______
14 직업의, 전문적인 ______
15 인식의, 인지의 ______
16 이용할 수 있는 ______
17 언급, 참조, 추천서 ______
18 회복시키다, 되찾다 ______
19 자산, 재산 ______
20 지적인, 지성을 갖춘 ______

C 다음 영어 단어의 유의어 또는 반의어를 쓰시오.

01 conversation = ________________

02 cause ↔ ________________

03 foster = ________________

04 trace = ________________

05 ability = ________________

06 restore = ________________

07 scatter ↔ ________________

08 massive ↔ ________________

09 multiple = ________________

10 asset = ________________

D 다음 문장의 빈칸에 주어진 철자로 시작하는 알맞은 단어를 쓰시오.

01 A supercomputer can suggest a__________ treatments for specific illnesses in an automated way.

슈퍼컴퓨터는 특정한 질병들에 대해 이용 가능한 치료법을 자동화된 방식으로 제안할 수 있다.

02 Ruben a__________ the client of theft after he refused to pay the full $3,500.

Ruben은 의뢰인이 3,500달러를 완전히 지불할 것을 거부한 후에 그를 절도죄로 고소했다.

03 An a__________ often given for sound is that of throwing a small stone onto the surface of a still pond.

소리 현상에 대해 자주 언급되는 비유는 작은 돌멩이를 고요한 연못 표면에 던지는 것이다.

04 Explicitly c__________ learning consists of a series of planned but weakly controlled experiments.

명백하게 인지적인 학습은 계획적이지만 약하게 통제되는 일련의 실험으로 구성된다.

05 This powerful capacity we all possess to some degree, is our ability to bend, not break, in the face of a__________.

우리 모두가 어느 정도 가지고 있는 이 강력한 능력은 역경에 직면하여 꺾이지 않고 구부러지는 우리의 능력이다.

06 E__________ pets are more likely to be wild animals that were caught and not bred in captivity to be domesticated.

이국적인 애완동물은 길들이기 위해 포획되어 사육되지 않은 야생 동물일 가능성이 더 크다.

A 다음 영어 단어에 해당하는 우리말 뜻을 쓰시오.

01 modern ______
02 drawback ______
03 destructive ______
04 possibility ______
05 steady ______
06 widespread ______
07 resemble ______
08 confront ______
09 reinforce ______
10 potential ______
11 decorate ______
12 contemporary ______
13 disadvantage ______
14 expertise ______
15 adolescence ______
16 integrate ______
17 strengthen ______
18 implement ______
19 identical ______
20 bring about ______

B 다음 우리말 뜻에 해당하는 영어 단어를 쓰시오.

01 계급(제), 지배층 ______
02 산업의, 공업의 ______
03 빈도, 진동(수) ______
04 원시의, 원시적인 ______
05 상담하다, 참고하다 ______
06 우세한, 지배적인 ______
07 관련된, 적절한 ______
08 붙이다, 첨부하다 ______
09 상호 간의 ______
10 가난, 빈곤 ______
11 ~의 관점에서 ______
12 열정적인, 열렬한 ______
13 긴급한, 시급한 ______
14 분명한, 솔직한 ______
15 부, 재산, 풍부 ______
16 근본적인, 필수적인 ______
17 분류하다, 구분하다 ______
18 복제하다, 번식하다 ______
19 승인하다, 찬성하다 ______
20 거주하다, 살다 ______

C 다음 영어 단어의 유의어 또는 반의어를 쓰시오.

01 explicit ↔ ________________

02 inhabit = ________________

03 steady = ________________

04 wealth ↔ ________________

05 resemble = ________________

06 mutual = ________________

07 reinforce ↔ ________________

08 classify = ________________

09 enthusiastic = ________________

10 dominant ↔ ________________

D 다음 문장의 빈칸에 주어진 철자로 시작하는 알맞은 단어를 쓰시오.

01 In c__________ culture, the benefits and drawbacks of multitasking are often discussed.
현대 문화에서, 다중 작업의 이점과 단점이 흔히 논의된다.

02 To check a given hypothesis, we need data r__________ to the hypothesis.
주어진 가설을 확인하기 위해 우리는 그 가설과 관련된 데이터가 필요하다.

03 With this, the function of the composer became i__________ into the recording process.
이와 함께 작곡가의 기능이 녹음 과정에 통합되었다.

04 H__________ is probably the most common form of organizing the workplace.
위계는 아마도 일터를 조직하는 가장 흔한 형태일 것이다.

05 Sickle cell is found in high f__________ in malarial regions.
낫 모양의 적혈구는 말라리아 지역에서 높은 빈도로 발견된다.

06 The mental experience of conscious free will may simply justify what our brains have already decided to i__________.
의식적인 자유 의지에 대한 정신적 경험은 우리의 뇌가 실행하기로 이미 결정한 것을 단순히 정당화하는 것일 수도 있다.

A 다음 영어 단어에 해당하는 우리말 뜻을 쓰시오.

01 glance ____________
02 resent ____________
03 ridiculous ____________
04 faithful ____________
05 sincere ____________
06 impulse ____________
07 responsible ____________
08 humiliate ____________
09 impatient ____________
10 genuine ____________
11 irritate ____________
12 tolerate ____________
13 jealous ____________
14 hesitate ____________
15 frustrated ____________
16 despair ____________
17 confident ____________
18 endure ____________
19 depression ____________
20 eager ____________

B 다음 우리말 뜻에 해당하는 영어 단어를 쓰시오.

01 솔직한, 숨김없는 ____________
02 서투른, 어색한 ____________
03 비참한, 불쌍한 ____________
04 불러일으키다 ____________
05 부끄러워하는 ____________
06 박수갈채 ____________
07 매료된, 매혹된 ____________
08 동정, 연민 ____________
09 깜짝 놀란 ____________
10 기어가다, 서행 ____________
11 기쁨, 기쁘게 하다 ____________
12 기대하다, 예상하다 ____________
13 관대한, 후한 ____________
14 겸손한, 비천한 ____________
15 거만한, 오만한 ____________
16 감정을 상하게 하다 ____________
17 감정 이입, 공감 ____________
18 ~을 참고 견디다 ____________
19 ~을 이해하다 ____________
20 (마음이) 내키지 않는 ____________

C 다음 영어 단어의 유의어 또는 반의어를 쓰시오.

01 sincere = __________

02 glance = __________

03 arrogant ↔ __________

04 put up with = __________

05 humiliate = __________

06 reluctant ↔ __________

07 arouse = __________

08 anticipate = __________

09 responsible ↔ __________

10 compassion = __________

D 다음 문장의 빈칸에 주어진 철자로 시작하는 알맞은 단어를 쓰시오.

01 Every time we learn, or remember, or m__________ __________ __________ something, we solve a problem.
우리가 무언가를 배우거나, 기억하거나, 이해할 때마다, 우리는 문제를 해결한다.

02 Regular consumption of energy drinks is associated with anxiety and d__________.
잦은 에너지 음료 소비는 불안 및 우울과 관련이 있다.

03 It can seem as if others are intentionally doing these things just to i__________ you.
마치 다른 사람들이 오직 당신을 화나게 하기 위해 일부러 이런 것들을 하고 있는 것처럼 보일 수 있다.

04 The capacity for e__________ is crucial to moral imagination.
공감 능력은 도덕적 상상에 매우 중요하다.

05 The students overcame their hesitation as they yelled r__________ answers to the teacher's questions.
학생들은 교사의 질문에 터무니없는 답변을 외치면서 자신들의 망설임을 극복했다.

06 Vincent van Gogh tried to remain f__________ to the original composition.
빈센트 반 고흐는 본래의 구도에 충실하려고 노력했다.

DAY 14

A 다음 영어 단어에 해당하는 우리말 뜻을 쓰시오.

01 collaborate	______	11 chief	______
02 procedure	______	12 attendant	______
03 bond	______	13 shift	______
04 strategy	______	14 deprive	______
05 withdraw	______	15 challenge	______
06 incentive	______	16 specialize	______
07 chore	______	17 familiar	______
08 occupation	______	18 rural	______
09 secure	______	19 strain	______
10 routine	______	20 miracle	______

B 다음 우리말 뜻에 해당하는 영어 단어를 쓰시오.

01 감독하다, 관리하다	______	11 먼, 외진, 원격의	______
02 동행하다, 수반하다	______	12 협상	______
03 환전, 교환하다	______	13 ~을 최대한 활용하다	______
04 결과, 성과	______	14 증명서, 자격증	______
05 모험	______	15 동반자, 동행	______
06 반응하다, 반작용하다	______	16 피난처, 보호하다	______
07 (직장) 동료	______	17 예금하다, 보증금	______
08 ~에 뒤처지지 않다	______	18 넘어서다, 초과하다	______
09 거주자, 거주하는	______	19 목적지, 도착지, 목표	______
10 도시의	______	20 복잡한	______

C 다음 영어 단어의 유의어 또는 반의어를 쓰시오.

01 supervise = ________________
02 withdraw ↔ ________________
03 familiar = ________________
04 exchange = ________________
05 urban ↔ ________________
06 remote = ________________
07 complicated = ________________
08 secure ↔ ________________
09 deprive = ________________
10 resident = ________________

D 다음 문장의 빈칸에 주어진 철자로 시작하는 알맞은 단어를 쓰시오.

01 These courses are for students wishing to s__________ in French cuisine.
이 강좌들은 프랑스 요리를 전문적으로 하고 싶어 하는 학생들을 위한 것이다.

02 We c__________ with local orphanages to protect unfortunate children.
우리는 불우한 아이들을 보호하기 위해서 현지 고아원과 협력한다.

03 Earning a reputation for being tough doesn't serve you well at the n__________ table.
강경하다는 평판을 얻는 것이 협상 테이블에서 여러분에게 도움이 되는 것은 아니다.

04 I waste too much time reading the latest gossip and k__________ __________ __________ my friends' updates.
나는 최신 가십 기사를 읽고 친구들의 최신 정보를 따라가는 데 너무 많은 시간을 낭비한다.

05 Kogi's marketing s__________ uses social networking to announce where it will turn up next.
Kogi의 마케팅 전략은 그것이 다음에 어디에서 나타날지를 알리기 위해 소셜 네트워킹을 사용한다.

06 The transportation industry has always done more than carry travelers from one d__________ to another.
운송 산업은 항상 한 목적지에서 다른 목적지로 이동하는 사람들을 실어 나르는 것 이상의 일을 해 왔다.

DAY 15

A 다음 영어 단어에 해당하는 우리말 뜻을 쓰시오.

01 dominate ____________

02 refund ____________

03 domestic ____________

04 ban ____________

05 sue ____________

06 imprison ____________

07 industrialize ____________

08 fund ____________

09 immigration ____________

10 commission ____________

11 owe ____________

12 govern ____________

13 property ____________

14 diplomat ____________

15 violate ____________

16 executive ____________

17 privilege ____________

18 suspect ____________

19 authority ____________

20 democracy ____________

B 다음 우리말 뜻에 해당하는 영어 단어를 쓰시오.

01 피난, 은신처 ____________

02 ~할 책임이 있는 ____________

03 ~에 상관없이 ____________

04 배포하다, 분배하다 ____________

05 타협하다, 손상시키다 ____________

06 정당화하다 ____________

07 분쟁, 논쟁하다 ____________

08 영토, 세력권 ____________

09 빚, 부채 ____________

10 목격자, 증언하다 ____________

11 상당하는, 동등한 것 ____________

12 급진적인, 과격한 ____________

13 특허권, 특허를 받다 ____________

14 지역, 지방, 영역 ____________

15 관리, 경영, 행정부 ____________

16 우선 사항, 우선권 ____________

17 후보자 ____________

18 상품, 물품 ____________

19 촉진하다, 승진시키다 ____________

20 (권력을) 행사하다 ____________

C 다음 영어 단어의 유의어 또는 반의어를 쓰시오.

01 immigration ↔ __________
02 dominate = __________
03 dispute = __________
04 domestic ↔ __________
05 violate = __________
06 property = __________
07 radical ↔ __________
08 commodity = __________
09 ban = __________
10 ban ↔ __________

D 다음 문장의 빈칸에 주어진 철자로 시작하는 알맞은 단어를 쓰시오.

01 They exercised all their power to make most of the settlers leave the t__________.
그들은 자신들의 모든 권력을 행사하여 대부분의 정착민들이 그 영토를 떠나도록 만들었다.

02 There are many talented e__________ with the ability to manage operations.
기업을 경영하는 능력을 지닌 재능 있는 중역들이 많이 있다.

03 There is a proper way to make an appeal to people who are in a__________ over us.
우리에 대한 권한이 있는 사람들에게 호소할 적절한 방법이 있다.

04 In general, ready meals are higher in fat than the homemade e__________.
대체로, 조리 가공된 식품은 집에서 만든 동등한 것보다 지방 함유량이 더 많다.

05 The judge has placed a p__________ on security above privacy.
그 판사는 사생활보다 안전을 우선으로 두어 왔다.

06 They want to d__________ as many supplies as possible to people in poor countries.
그들은 가난한 국가의 사람들에게 가능한 한 많은 보급품을 배포하고 싶어 한다.

DAY 16

A 다음 영어 단어에 해당하는 우리말 뜻을 쓰시오.

01 liquid ______
02 volcanic ______
03 organism ______
04 skeleton ______
05 species ______
06 astronomy ______
07 temperature ______
08 vapor ______
09 tissue ______
10 predator ______
11 mixture ______
12 particle ______
13 migrate ______
14 mammal ______
15 gravity ______
16 stem ______
17 extract ______
18 burst ______
19 layer ______
20 fluid ______

B 다음 우리말 뜻에 해당하는 영어 단어를 쓰시오.

01 가설, 가정 ______
02 서식지, 주거지 ______
03 나뭇가지, 지점 ______
04 금속 ______
05 ~을 생각해 내다 ______
06 실험실, 실험용의 ______
07 살아남다, 생존하다 ______
08 기체, 가솔린 ______
09 빙하 ______
10 ~으로 이루어지다 ______
11 빛, 광선 ______
12 A가 ~하는 것을 막다 ______
13 방법, 수단 ______
14 떨다, 진동하다 ______
15 고체, 견고한 ______
16 성분, 부품, 구성하는 ______
17 신경 ______
18 분자, 미량 ______
19 관찰, 관측 ______
20 독성의, 유독한 ______

C 다음 영어 단어의 유의어 또는 반의어를 쓰시오.

01 burst	= ______	05 branch	= ______
02 fluid	= ______	06 ray	= ______
03 predator	↔ ______	07 consist of	= ______
04 organism	= ______	08 component	= ______

D 다음 문장의 빈칸에 주어진 철자로 시작하는 알맞은 단어를 쓰시오.

01 In a l______ setting, experiments are carefully designed to generate the needed data.

실험실 환경에서, 실험은 그 필요한 데이터를 생성하기 위해 세심하게 설계된다.

02 If you have been the victim of t______ exposure, please contact us for a free consultation.

만약 당신이 독성 노출의 피해자라면, 무료 상담을 위해 우리에게 연락하세요.

03 To a p______ physicist, motion backward in time is not that confusing.

입자 물리학자에게 시간이 거꾸로 흐르는 것은 그렇게 혼란스러운 것이 아니다.

04 No species can detect all the m______ that are present in the environment in which it lives.

어떤 종도 그것이 살고 있는 환경에 존재하는 모든 분자들을 감지할 수는 없다.

05 The air seemed to v______ with tension as it got close to the wire.

최후의 순간이 가까워지면서 분위기는 긴장으로 떨리는 것 같았다.

06 It set the stage for innovation and discovery, for c______ ______ ______ something new.

그것은 새로운 것을 생각해 내는 혁신과 발견의 장을 마련해 주었다.

DAY 17

A 다음 영어 단어에 해당하는 우리말 뜻을 쓰시오.

01 prejudice ______
02 spirit ______
03 ascend ______
04 tragic ______
05 context ______
06 comic ______
07 profound ______
08 myth ______
09 paradoxically ______
10 outline ______
11 modify ______
12 shallow ______
13 colonial ______
14 plot ______
15 bias ______
16 humanity ______
17 absolute ______
18 oppose ______
19 noble ______
20 ironically ______

B 다음 우리말 뜻에 해당하는 영어 단어를 쓰시오.

01 물질, 본질 ______
02 철학 ______
03 철자를 쓰다, 마법 ______
04 비유, 은유 ______
05 초안, 밑그림 ______
06 ~을 고려하다 ______
07 단순화하다 ______
08 권능을 주다 ______
09 궁극적인, 최고의 ______
10 유산 ______
11 함축하다, 암시하다 ______
12 인공의, 인위적인 ______
13 의식, 의례적인 ______
14 정복하다, 이기다 ______
15 연속, 시리즈 ______
16 내재하는, 고유의 ______
17 전통적인, 관습적인 ______
18 번역하다 ______
19 ~에서 유래하다 ______
20 소설, 허구 ______

C 다음 영어 단어의 유의어 또는 반의어를 쓰시오.

01 heritage	= ________	06 metaphor	= ________
02 shallow	↔ ________	07 empower	= ________
03 ritual	= ________	08 ironically	= ________
04 conventional	= ________	09 comic	↔ ________
05 simplify	↔ ________	10 inherent	= ________

D 다음 문장의 빈칸에 주어진 철자로 시작하는 알맞은 단어를 쓰시오.

01 Diet sodas replace the sugar with a________ sweeteners.
다이어트 탄산음료는 설탕을 인공 감미료로 대체한다.

02 Is there anybody who can t________ this into Spanish?
이것을 스페인어로 번역할 수 있는 사람이 있나요?

03 All the bad deeds committed by the country under its c________ rule were on display.
식민지 통치하에서 그 나라에 의해 자행된 모든 악행들이 전시되었다.

04 The term is d________ ________ the 15th-century Medici family, who helped usher in the Renaissance.
그 용어는 15세기 메디치 가문에서 유래하는데, 그들은 르네상스 시대가 시작되도록 도왔다.

05 Every human being is affected by unconscious b________ that lead us to make incorrect assumptions about other people.
모든 인간은 다른 사람들에 대한 부정확한 추측을 하도록 이끄는 무의식적인 편견에 의해 영향을 받는다.

06 It is important to guess their meanings from the c________ in which idioms are used.
관용어는 그것들이 사용된 맥락을 통해 의미를 추측하는 것이 중요하다.

DAY 18

A 다음 영어 단어에 해당하는 우리말 뜻을 쓰시오.

01 portrait	______	11 external	______
02 abstract	______	12 popularity	______
03 amuse	______	13 impressive	______
04 elaborate	______	14 entrance	______
05 coordinate	______	15 institute	______
06 harmonize	______	16 rehearse	______
07 theme	______	17 imaginative	______
08 authentic	______	18 entertain	______
09 creative	______	19 encounter	______
10 orchestra	______	20 flash	______

B 다음 우리말 뜻에 해당하는 영어 단어를 쓰시오.

01 건축가	______	11 내부의	______
02 걸작, 명작	______	12 다르다	______
03 고전의, 클래식의	______	13 닦다, 윤[광]내다	______
04 공연하다, 실행하다	______	14 대비, 대조를 이루다	______
05 공예, 공들여 만들다	______	15 마법의	______
06 구별하다, 식별하다	______	16 무너지다, 붕괴하다	______
07 구성하다, 작곡하다	______	17 비율, 부분, 균형	______
08 구체적인, 콘크리트	______	18 사회화하다, 교제하다	______
09 귀중한, 소중한	______	19 (~에서) 역할을 하다	______
10 기념물, 기념의	______	20 ~와 관련[연관]되다	______

C 다음 영어 단어의 유의어 또는 반의어를 쓰시오.

01 amuse ⊜ ____________

02 entrance ↔ ____________

03 memorial ⊜ ____________

04 abstract ↔ ____________

05 precious ⊜ ____________

06 impressive ⊜ ____________

07 internal ↔ ____________

08 distinguish ⊜ ____________

D 다음 문장의 빈칸에 주어진 철자로 시작하는 알맞은 단어를 쓰시오.

01 To develop your c__________ thinking skills, try to look at things from a new perspective.
창의적인 사고 능력을 계발하기 위해서는, 새로운 관점으로 사물을 보도록 노력하라.

02 His attempt turned out to be a very e__________ one.
그의 시도는 매우 공을 들인 것으로 밝혀졌다.

03 Collectors seek a__________ originals with provenance because they are more valuable.
수집가들은 진짜 원본들이 더 가치 있기 때문에 출처가 있는 진짜 원본들을 찾는다.

04 Let's c__________ with local police to address the problem.
그 문제를 처리하기 위해 현지 경찰과 조정을 합시다.

05 An i__________ idea might rise to the surface in only a second.
상상력이 풍부한 아이디어는 단 1초 만에 수면 위로 올라올 수도 있다.

06 Whatever the p__________ of a work's showing to telling, there is always something for readers to interpret.
작품의 보여 주기 대 말하기의 비율이 어떻든지 간에, 독자가 해석해야 하는 무언가가 항상 존재한다.

A 다음 영어 단어에 해당하는 우리말 뜻을 쓰시오.

01 minimize ______

02 multiply ______

03 commute ______

04 install ______

05 rush ______

06 automatic ______

07 passenger ______

08 transport ______

09 visual ______

10 equation ______

11 sort ______

12 loosen ______

13 inspect ______

14 crash ______

15 virtual ______

16 angle ______

17 recharge ______

18 electronic ______

19 navigate ______

20 spare ______

B 다음 우리말 뜻에 해당하는 영어 단어를 쓰시오.

01 통계, 통계 자료 ______

02 다운로드하다 ______

03 항공기 ______

04 부딪치다, 혹 ______

05 거친, 대강의 ______

06 활성화시키다 ______

07 조립하다, 모으다 ______

08 수송, 선적, 수송품 ______

09 (탈것을) 타다 ______

10 다수의, 수많은 ______

11 업로드하다 ______

12 기계의, 역학의 ______

13 우주 비행사 ______

14 가속하다, 촉진하다 ______

15 수동의, 설명서 ______

16 원자력의, 핵의 ______

17 최대화하다 ______

18 회로, 순환 ______

19 A를 공통점으로 가지다 ______

20 A를 B로 바꾸다 ______

C 다음 영어 단어의 유의어 또는 반의어를 쓰시오.

01 rough ⊜ ____________

02 install ⊜ ____________

03 upload ↔ ____________

04 numerous ⊜ ____________

05 maximize ↔ ____________

06 spare ⊜ ____________

07 manual ↔ ____________

08 sort ⊜ ____________

09 inspect ⊜ ____________

10 loosen ↔ ____________

D 다음 문장의 빈칸에 주어진 철자로 시작하는 알맞은 단어를 쓰시오.

01 Physical bookstores simply could not stock as many titles as a v__________ bookstore could.
물리적인 서점은 결코 가상 서점이 할 수 있는 만큼 많은 서적을 구비할 수 없었다.

02 Mae C. Jemison was named the first black woman a__________ in 1987.
Mae C. Jemison은 1987년에 최초의 흑인 여성 우주 비행사로 임명되었다.

03 Countless species of animals manage to n__________ the world, solve problems, and learn without using language.
수많은 종의 동물들이 언어를 사용하지 않고도 세계를 항해하고, 문제를 해결하고, 학습해 낸다.

04 When we listen to words conveying painful thoughts, our brains a__________ to feel that pain.
우리가 고통스러운 생각을 전달하는 말을 들었을 때, 우리의 뇌는 그 고통을 느끼는 것을 활성화시킨다.

05 A loud engine noise filled the air with its heavy m__________ sounds.
시끄러운 엔진 소리가 그것의 거대한 기계음으로 대기를 채웠다.

06 The brake systems t__________ some drivers __________ markedly inferior drivers.
그 브레이크 시스템은 일부 운전자들을 눈에 띄게 열등한 운전자들로 바꾸었다.

DAY 20

A 다음 영어 단어에 해당하는 우리말 뜻을 쓰시오.

01 cure	________	11 recipe	________
02 track	________	12 heal	________
03 stretch	________	13 row	________
04 therapy	________	14 symptom	________
05 stroke	________	15 spill	________
06 fatigue	________	16 nutrient	________
07 bleed	________	17 suffer from	________
08 scent	________	18 portion	________
09 stir	________	19 pregnant	________
10 posture	________	20 flexible	________

B 다음 우리말 뜻에 해당하는 영어 단어를 쓰시오.

01 처방하다	________	11 극심한, 극단	________
02 수술, 외과	________	12 맛, 풍미, 향미(료)	________
03 숨, 호흡	________	13 만성적인, 장기간의	________
04 섬유, 섬유질	________	14 진단하다	________
05 면역성의	________	15 반대자, 경기 상대	________
06 먹을 수 있는	________	16 ~에 영향을 미치다	________
07 굶주리다, 갈망하다	________	17 목표, 겨냥하다	________
08 소화, 소화력	________	18 식이요법의	________
09 기절하다, 희미한	________	19 신체의, 물질적인	________
10 근육, 근력	________	20 비만	________

C 다음 영어 단어의 유의어 또는 반의어를 쓰시오.

01 flavor = ____________

02 cure = ____________

03 physical ↔ ____________

04 faint = ____________

05 edible ↔ ____________

06 opponent = ____________

07 chronic ↔ ____________

08 target = ____________

D 다음 문장의 빈칸에 주어진 철자로 시작하는 알맞은 단어를 쓰시오.

01 Increased muscle strength will improve your balance when maintaining difficult yoga p__________.
증가된 근력은 어려운 요가 자세를 유지할 때 균형을 향상시킬 것이다.

02 Sometimes, their works confuse us with their e__________ reality.
때때로 그들의 작품은 그것이 가진 극도의 현실성으로 우리를 혼란스럽게 한다.

03 Music can help improve the functioning of your i__________ system.
음악은 여러분의 면역 체계의 기능을 향상시키는 데 도움을 줄 수 있다.

04 Monet s__________ __________ cataracts for much of his later life.
Monet는 그의 말년의 많은 시간을 백내장으로 고통받았다.

05 Those foods rarely contain the n__________ needed to support body functions.
그런 음식들은 몸의 기능을 지탱하는 데 필요한 영양소를 거의 포함하고 있지 않다.

06 D__________ supplements are products designed to give you nutrients that might be missing from your diet.
음식[식이] 보충제는 여러분의 식단에서 빠질 수 있는 영양소를 여러분에게 주기 위해 고안된 제품이다.

DAY 21

A 다음 영어 단어에 해당하는 우리말 뜻을 쓰시오.

01 evaluate ________
02 typical ________
03 voluntary ________
04 grant ________
05 policy ________
06 admire ________
07 argue ________
08 intermediate ________
09 guidance ________
10 intellectual ________
11 assist ________
12 invade ________
13 inevitable ________
14 pupil ________
15 academic ________
16 discipline ________
17 aid ________
18 award ________
19 assess ________
20 strict ________

B 다음 우리말 뜻에 해당하는 영어 단어를 쓰시오.

01 악보, 점수, 득점하다 ________
02 ~에서 기인하다 ________
03 발표, 설명, 제출 ________
04 가르치다, 지시하다 ________
05 감사 ________
06 고립시키다 ________
07 공식적인, 형식적인 ________
08 괴롭히다, 성가심 ________
09 집단의, 공동의 ________
10 변장하다, 위장 ________
11 등록하다 ________
12 명령하다, 통솔 ________
13 모집하다, 신병 ________
14 ~을 제거하다 ________
15 유발하다, 방아쇠 ________
16 범위, (~에) 이르다 ________
17 사로잡힌, 감금된 ________
18 상호 작용하다 ________
19 설명, 해명 ________
20 시도하다, 시도 ________

C 다음 영어 단어의 유의어 또는 반의어를 쓰시오.

01 recruit ⊜ ______________

02 inevitable ⊜ ______________

03 grant ⊜ ______________

04 collective ↔ ______________

05 get rid of ⊜ ______________

06 explanation ⊜ ______________

07 bother ⊜ ______________

08 formal ↔ ______________

09 evaluate ⊜ ______________

10 assist ⊜ ______________

D 다음 문장의 빈칸에 주어진 철자로 시작하는 알맞은 단어를 쓰시오.

01 I want to extend my g__________ to my parents for their love and sacrifice.
나는 부모님의 사랑과 희생에 대해 그분들께 감사를 드리고 싶다.

02 He took a special interest in his son's i__________ development.
그는 자신의 아들의 지적 발달에 특별한 관심을 가졌다.

03 When you i__________ with other people, there are times when we need to use humor.
여러분이 다른 사람들과 교류할 때, 우리는 유머를 사용해야 할 때도 있다.

04 Your smartphone apps can i__________ your privacy.
여러분의 스마트폰 앱이 여러분의 사생활을 침해할 수 있다.

05 I was ready for the i__________ swimming class after months of taking the beginner courses.
나는 초급 코스를 몇 개월 동안 수강한 후 중급 수영반에 들어갈 준비가 되었다.

06 We all have unpleasant memories of being d__________ when we were children.
우리 모두는 어렸을 때 훈육을 받은 유쾌하지 않은 기억을 가지고 있다.

DAY 22

A 다음 영어 단어에 해당하는 우리말 뜻을 쓰시오.

01 frightened ____________

02 convince ____________

03 psychology ____________

04 relief ____________

05 stable ____________

06 interfere ____________

07 innate ____________

08 curiosity ____________

09 persuade ____________

10 attribute ____________

11 intend ____________

12 assumption ____________

13 sudden ____________

14 intervene ____________

15 overwhelm ____________

16 associate ____________

17 afraid ____________

18 cheat ____________

19 stress ____________

20 favorable ____________

B 다음 우리말 뜻에 해당하는 영어 단어를 쓰시오.

01 절박한, 필사적인 ____________

02 환영, 환상, 착각 ____________

03 무지한, 무식한 ____________

04 불안, 걱정, 염려 ____________

05 불안한, 불편한 ____________

06 결국 ~이 되다 ____________

07 확인하다, 동일시하다 ____________

08 집중을 방해하는 것 ____________

09 낙관적인, 낙관하는 ____________

10 회의적인, 의심 많은 ____________

11 상황에 맞지 않은 ____________

12 주관적인, 주관의 ____________

13 짐, ~에게 짐을 지우다 ____________

14 제외하다, 배제하다 ____________

15 경험하다, 겪다 ____________

16 보장하다, 확보하다 ____________

17 복잡한, 콤플렉스 ____________

18 정신의, 지적인 ____________

19 북돋우다, 증가 ____________

20 조종하다 ____________

C 다음 영어 단어의 유의어 또는 반의어를 쓰시오.

01 persuade = ____________

02 subjective ↔ ____________

03 innate = ____________

04 attribute = ____________

05 complex ↔ ____________

06 interfere = ____________

07 anxiety = ____________

08 favorable ↔ ____________

09 sudden = ____________

10 exclude ↔ ____________

D 다음 문장의 빈칸에 주어진 철자로 시작하는 알맞은 단어를 쓰시오.

01 How do you know if someone is m__________ you?

누군가가 당신을 교묘히 조종하고 있는지 아닌지를 어떻게 알겠는가?

02 The rhythm that frequency generates allows stressors to be i__________.

맥박수가 만들어 내는 리듬은 스트레스 원인들을 확인할 수 있게 한다.

03 The elderly woman was d__________ and could not find any other means of transport.

그 할머니는 절박했고 다른 운송 수단을 찾을 수가 없었다.

04 The resource is o__________ and competitors are excluded by sheer weight of numbers.

순전히 수적 우위에 의해 자원이 압도되고 경쟁자들이 배제된다.

05 Classrooms with too much decoration are a source of d__________ for young children.

너무 많은 장식이 있는 교실이 어린이들의 주의 산만의 원인이다.

06 Remember that being s__________ does you no good.

회의적인 것이 당신에게 아무런 득이 되지 않는다는 것을 기억하라.

DAY 23

A 다음 영어 단어에 해당하는 우리말 뜻을 쓰시오.

01 announce	______	11 deliver	______
02 diminish	______	12 audience	______
03 enhance	______	13 variable	______
04 leak	______	14 lessen	______
05 pile	______	15 mobile	______
06 viewer	______	16 verbal	______
07 broadcast	______	17 appealing	______
08 brief	______	18 medium	______
09 transaction	______	19 visible	______
10 portable	______	20 satellite	______

B 다음 우리말 뜻에 해당하는 영어 단어를 쓰시오.

01 칼럼, 기둥	______	11 일, 문제, 사건	______
02 제한, 한계	______	12 신호를 보내다, 암시하다	______
03 광고, 상업의	______	13 봉투	______
04 분명한, 눈에 띄는	______	14 조합, 연합, 동맹	______
05 분명치 않은, 모호한	______	15 ~와 연락[접촉]하다	______
06 정보를 주는, 유익한	______	16 우표, 발을 구르다	______
07 응답자	______	17 수집하다, 수신자 부담의	______
08 자유롭게 ~하다	______	18 싸다, 포장하다	______
09 설명하다, 삽화를 넣다	______	19 보내다, 전염시키다	______
10 설득력 있는	______	20 전(달)하다, 운반하다	______

C 다음 영어 단어의 유의어 또는 반의어를 쓰시오.

01 enhance = ____________

02 viewer = ____________

03 union = ____________

04 appealing = ____________

05 evident ↔ ____________

06 convey = ____________

07 visible ↔ ____________

08 informative = ____________

09 mobile ↔ ____________

10 limitation = ____________

D 다음 문장의 빈칸에 주어진 철자로 시작하는 알맞은 단어를 쓰시오.

01 He thought nonverbal and v__________ skills might retain their strong ties.
그는 비언어적 기술과 언어적 기술이 그들의 강한 유대감을 유지할 수 있을 거라고 생각했다.

02 A one-way mirror t__________ half the light and reflects the other half.
단방향 거울은 절반의 빛은 투과시키고 나머지 반은 반사시킨다.

03 Advertisements cover cars and buildings and TV c__________ shout slogans.
광고들이 자동차와 건물을 덮고 TV 광고들은 슬로건을 외친다.

04 We will hardly notice those advertisements that seemed so c__________ just moments earlier.
우리는 바로 조금 전에 매우 강력해 보였던 광고들을 거의 알아차리지 못할 것이다.

05 The first artificial s__________, Sputnik I, was launched on Oct. 4, 1957.
최초의 인공위성인 스푸트니크 1호는 1957년 10월 4일에 발사되었다.

06 Scientists can change the satellites' orbital positions by taking all v__________ into account.
과학자들은 모든 변수를 고려하여 위성의 궤도 위치를 변경할 수 있다.

DAY 24

A 다음 영어 단어에 해당하는 우리말 뜻을 쓰시오.

01 endangered ____________
02 convert ____________
03 utilize ____________
04 discard ____________
05 incline ____________
06 fragile ____________
07 wasteful ____________
08 steep ____________
09 conserve ____________
10 remain ____________
11 fossil ____________
12 peak ____________
13 straw ____________
14 transform ____________
15 dispose of ____________
16 generate ____________
17 raw ____________
18 atmosphere ____________
19 acid ____________
20 purify ____________

B 다음 우리말 뜻에 해당하는 영어 단어를 쓰시오.

01 표면, 수면으로 올라오다 ____________
02 자원, 물자 ____________
03 여과 장치, 거르다 ____________
04 풍경, 경치 ____________
05 적절한, 적합한 ____________
06 열대 우림 ____________
07 쓰레기, 버리다 ____________
08 살충제 ____________
09 재활용하다 ____________
10 쓰레기 매립지 ____________
11 절벽 ____________
12 줄이다, 감소시키다 ____________
13 아마 ~일 것이다 ____________
14 축적하다, 모으다 ____________
15 위협하다, 협박하다 ____________
16 생태계 ____________
17 쓸다, 휩쓸다, 쓸기 ____________
18 소중히 하다 ____________
19 직물, 천 ____________
20 오염 ____________

C 다음 영어 단어의 유의어 또는 반의어를 쓰시오.

01 raw ↔ ______________

02 suitable = ______________

03 litter = ______________

04 surface = ______________

05 threaten = ______________

06 incline ↔ ______________

07 landscape = ______________

08 convert = ______________

09 pollution = ______________

10 purify ↔ ______________

D 다음 문장의 빈칸에 주어진 철자로 시작하는 알맞은 단어를 쓰시오.

01 Koreans d__________ __________ over 15 billion cups each year.
한국인들은 매년 150억 개가 넘는 컵을 버린다.

02 Stronger, taller vegetables grow above smaller, more f__________ vegetables.
더 튼튼하고 키가 큰 채소들은 더 작고 연약한 채소들 위에서 자란다.

03 We can reduce the amount of trash thrown away and c__________ natural resources by recycling.
우리는 재활용을 통해 버려지는 쓰레기의 양을 줄일 수 있고, 천연자원을 보존할 수 있다.

04 Microplastics that a__________ in the body are a source of chemical contamination to tissues and fluids.
몸에 축적되는 미세 플라스틱은 조직과 체액에 화학적 오염의 원천이다.

05 They become pollutants only when the coal is burned and the combustion products are released into the a__________.
그것들은 석탄이 타고 연소 생성물이 대기에 배출될 때만 오염 물질이 된다.

06 Man-made disasters have destroyed vital e__________.
인간이 만든 재앙들이 핵심 생태계를 파괴해 왔다.

DAY 25

A 다음 영어 단어에 해당하는 우리말 뜻을 쓰시오.

01 drain ____________
02 climate ____________
03 hatch ____________
04 melt ____________
05 agriculture ____________
06 take over ____________
07 float ____________
08 cultivate ____________
09 fierce ____________
10 temperate ____________
11 enrich ____________
12 harvest ____________
13 shadow ____________
14 durable ____________
15 drought ____________
16 crop ____________
17 fertile ____________
18 light ____________
19 folk ____________
20 intense ____________

B 다음 우리말 뜻에 해당하는 영어 단어를 쓰시오.

01 ~을 이용[활용]하다 ____________
02 토착의, 원산의, 원주민 ____________
03 열대의, 열대 지방의 ____________
04 현상 ____________
05 창조물, 생물 ____________
06 유래[발생]하다, 고안하다 ____________
07 습한, 습기 찬 ____________
08 익은, 숙성한 ____________
09 얼다, 동결시키다 ____________
10 해충, 골칫거리 ____________
11 연례의, 연간의 ____________
12 충분한 ____________
13 척박한, 결실이 없는 ____________
14 지진 ____________
15 폭발, 분화 ____________
16 저항력이 있는, 잘 견디는 ____________
17 조수(潮水), 조류, 흐름 ____________
18 파도, 파도치다, 흔들다 ____________
19 잡초, 잡초를 제거하다 ____________
20 옮겨 심다, 이식하다, 이식 ____________

C 다음 영어 단어의 유의어 또는 반의어를 쓰시오.

01 intense	=	____________	06 float	↔	____________
02 barren	↔	____________	07 temperate	=	____________
03 freeze	↔	____________	08 cultivate	=	____________
04 sufficient	=	____________	09 durable	↔	____________
05 originate	=	____________	10 harvest	=	____________

D 다음 문장의 빈칸에 주어진 철자로 시작하는 알맞은 단어를 쓰시오.

01 Try wearing a couple of extra jackets on a hot h__________ day and run a mile.
덥고 습한 날에 여분의 재킷 두 개를 입는 것을 시도하고 1마일을 뛰어라.

02 These crops are r__________ to some of the major infectious diseases.
이 작물들은 몇 가지 주요 전염병에 저항력이 있다.

03 This fierce fish is usually found in warm, t__________ seas.
이 사나운 물고기는 대개 따뜻한 열대 바다에서 발견된다.

04 India's increase in a__________ water demand is expected to lead the other regions'.
인도의 연간 물 수요의 증가량이 다른 지역의 증가량을 앞설 것으로 예상된다.

05 Volcanic e__________ and earthquakes occur very often in Indonesia.
인도네시아에서는 화산 폭발과 지진이 매우 자주 발생한다.

06 This p__________ causes the stem to bend and appear to be growing towards the light.
이 현상은 줄기가 휘어지게 하고 빛을 향하여 성장하는 것처럼 보이게 한다.

DAY 26

Ⓐ 다음 빈칸에 알맞은 영어 단어나 우리말 뜻을 쓰시오.

01	________	① 발달하다, 발달시키다 ④ (필름을) 현상하다	② 개발하다	③ 생기다, 발생하다
02	air	① ________ ④ ________	② ________	③ ________
03	________	① 확인[검사]하다, 검사	② 수표	③ 계산서
04	regard	① ________ ④ ________	② ________	③ ________
05	yield	① ________	② ________	③ ________
06	________	① 사물, 물체 ④ 반대하다	② 목표, 목적	③ 대상
07	________	① 조용한 ④ 그럼에도 불구하고	② 정지한	③ 훨씬, 더욱
08	custom	① ________	② ________	③ ________
09	account	① ________ ④ ________	② ________	③ ________
10	________	① 맞는, 올바른	② 정정하다, 바로잡다	
11	________	① (뾰족한) 끝	② 조언	③ 팁, 사례금
12	charge	① ________ ④ ________	② ________	③ ________

B 다음 영어 단어에 해당하는 우리말 뜻을 쓰시오.

01 mass	______	06 cite	______
02 mess	______	07 site	______
03 literal	______	08 optical	______
04 literate	______	09 optional	______
05 literary	______	10 optimal	______

C 다음 문장의 괄호 안에서 문맥상 알맞은 것을 고르시오.

01 In ancient Egypt, cats were considered **[sacred / scared]**, and the punishment for killing one was death.
고대 이집트에서, 고양이들은 신성하게 여겨졌으며, 고양이를 죽이는 것에 대한 벌은 사형이었다.

02 He **[expends / expands]** most of his energy on creating literature.
그는 자신의 에너지 대부분을 문학 창작에 쓴다.

03 Most insect species would have long since become **[instinct / extinct]**.
대부분의 곤충 종은 오래전에 멸종했을 것이다.

04 After **[considerable / considerate]** argument, they convinced Zelter that their plan would work.
상당한 논쟁 후에, 그들은 자신들의 계획이 효과가 있을 것이라고 Zelter를 납득시켰다

05 A severe **[feminine / famine]** in Africa drove many Africans to relief camps throughout the continent.
아프리카의 극심한 기근은 많은 아프리카인들을 대륙 전역에 걸쳐 있는 구호 수용소로 이동하게 했다.

06 Antonie van Leeuwenhoek was known **[as / for]** his cell research.
Antonie van Leeuwenhoek는 그의 세포 연구로 유명했다.

DAY 27

Ⓐ 다음 빈칸에 알맞은 영어 단어나 우리말 뜻을 쓰시오.

01	contract	① ________ ② ________ ③ ________
02	________	① 소리, 소리를 내다 ② ~인 것 같다, ~처럼 들리다 ③ 건전한 ④ 깊게, 푹
03	bill	① ________ ② ________ ③ ________ ④ ________
04	character	① ________ ② ________ ③ ________ ④ ________
05	________	① 곰 ② 참다, 견디다 ③ 낳다, (열매를) 맺다
06	________	① 균형을 잡다, 균형 ② 잔고, 잔액 ③ 저울
07	________	① 주제 ② 과목, 학과 ③ 피실험자 ④ ~을 받기 쉬운, ~될 수 있는
08	count	① ________ ② ________ ③ ________
09	________	① (선으로) 그리다 ② 끌어당기다 ③ (관심을) 끌다 ④ (결론을) 내다[도출하다]
10	grave	① ________ ② ________ ③ ________
11	present	① ________ ② ________ ③ ________ ④ ________
12	________	① 잡고[쥐고] 있다, 들다 ② 개최하다, 열다 ③ 두다, 유지하다 ④ 담다, 수용하다

B 다음 영어 단어에 해당하는 우리말 뜻을 쓰시오.

01 principal ____________

02 principle ____________

03 defeat ____________

04 defect ____________

05 frame ____________

06 flame ____________

07 carve ____________

08 curve ____________

09 absorb ____________

10 absurd ____________

C 다음 문장의 괄호 안에서 문맥상 알맞은 것을 고르시오.

01 His help will be a strong **[compliment / complement]** to our team.
그의 도움은 우리 팀에게 강력한 보완책이 될 것이다.

02 More than half of all stock orders placed by individuals in the United States were **[imitated / initiated]** via the Internet.
미국에서 개인에 의해 발주된 모든 주식 주문의 절반 이상이 인터넷을 통해 시작되었다.

03 The lecture was about the **[respective / respectable]** roles of men and women in society.
그 강연은 사회에서 남성과 여성 각자의 역할에 대한 것이었다.

04 Ancestral humans lost their hair over **[successive / successful]** generations.
인간 조상들은 잇따른 세대에 걸쳐서 털을 잃었다.

05 This car has many mechanical **[defects / defeats]**.
이 자동차는 기계적인 결함이 많다.

06 There are many evolutionary or cultural reasons for **[corporation / cooperation]**.
협동에 대한 진화적이거나 문화적인 이유가 많이 있다.

DAY 28

A 다음 빈칸에 알맞은 영어 단어나 우리말 뜻을 쓰시오.

01	fine	① ______	② ______	③ ______
		④ ______		
02	current	① ______	② ______	③ ______
		④ ______		
03	______	① 기간	② 학기	③ 용어
		④ 사이, 관계	⑤ 조건	
04	solution	① ______	② ______	
05	______	① 책, 서적	② 예약하다	
06	rate	① ______	② ______	③ ______
		④ ______		
07	______	① 공평한, 공정한	② 상당한	③ 아름다운, 매력적인
		④ (날씨가) 맑은	⑤ 박람회	
08	______	① 수행하다	② 지휘하다	③ 안내하다, 안내
		④ (열·전기를) 전도하다	⑤ 행동	
09	critical	① ______	② ______	③ ______
10	______	① 누르다	② 강요하다, 재촉하다	③ 언론, 출판
11	feature	① ______	② ______	③ ______
12	condition	① ______	② ______	③ ______

B 다음 영어 단어에 해당하는 우리말 뜻을 쓰시오.

01 conscience	________________	06 rise	________________
02 conscious	________________	07 personal	________________
03 emergency	________________	08 personnel	________________
04 emergence	________________	09 depend	________________
05 raise	________________	10 defend	________________

C 다음 문장의 괄호 안에서 문맥상 알맞은 것을 고르시오.

01 The death of languages is merely a sign of the gradual **[revolution / evolution]**.
언어의 사멸은 단지 점진적인 진화의 한 표시일 뿐이다.

02 The model will be used to **[simulate / stimulate]** the effects of an earthquake.
그 모형은 지진의 영향들을 모의 실험하는 데 사용될 것이다.

03 Explain to the child why his behavior must **[confirm / conform]** to family norms.
아이의 행동이 가족의 규범을 따라야 하는 이유를 아이에게 설명하라.

04 Gestures and speech used similar **[neural / neutral]** circuits as they developed in our evolutionary history.
몸짓과 언어는 우리의 진화 역사에서 발달할 때 유사한 신경 회로를 사용했다.

05 The program **[calculates / circulates]** the number of days between any two dates.
그 프로그램은 두 날짜 사이의 일수를 계산한다.

06 It should be concerned **[about / with]** your safety and security.
그것은 당신의 안전 및 보안과 관련이 있어야 한다.

DAY 29

A 다음 빈칸에 알맞은 영어 단어나 우리말 뜻을 쓰시오.

01	________	① 감소하다, 하락하다, 감소, 하락 ② 거절하다 ③ 아래로 경사지다, 아래를 향하다
02	suit	① ________ ② ________ ③ ________
03	correspond	① ________ ② ________ ③ ________ ④ ________
04	________	① 해산시키다 ② 해고하다 ③ (생각 등을) 떨쳐 버리다
05	________	① 기둥 ② 우편, 우편물 ③ 붙이다, 게시하다 ④ (우편물을) 발송하다
06	case	① ________ ② ________ ③ ________ ④ ________
07	article	① ________ ② ________ ③ ________
08	________	① 예약하다 ② 따로 남겨 두다 ③ 보유하다 ④ 매장량, 비축 ⑤ 보호 구역
09	________	① 함께 있는 사람들, 친구 ② 동석, 동행 ③ 회사
10	reflect	① ________ ② ________ ③ ________
11	appreciate	① ________ ② ________ ③ ________
12	________	① 수치 ② 모습, 몸매 ③ 인물, 사람 ④ 모양, 무늬 ⑤ 이해하다, 생각해 내다

B 다음 영어 단어에 해당하는 우리말 뜻을 쓰시오.

01 state ______________

02 statue ______________

03 status ______________

04 waist ______________

05 waste ______________

06 saw ______________

07 sew ______________

08 sow ______________

09 hospitality ______________

10 hostility ______________

C 다음 문장의 괄호 안에서 문맥상 알맞은 것을 고르시오.

01 They lack the **[ethical / ethnic]** considerations that trained journalists have.
그들은 훈련받은 언론인들이 가지고 있는 윤리적인 생각이 부족하다.

02 Human companions can display **[constant / consistent]** emotional support.
사람 친구는 일관된 정서적 지지를 보일 수 있다.

03 Lightning **[precedes / proceeds]** the thunder because light travels faster than sound.
빛이 소리보다 더 빠르게 이동하기 때문에 번개는 천둥에 앞선다.

04 There have been stories all over the media about online game **[addition / addiction]**.
온라인 게임 중독에 대한 이야기들이 미디어 곳곳에 있어 왔다.

05 The department will try to find someone to **[substitute / constitute]** for you.
그 부서는 당신을 대신할 사람을 찾으려고 할 것이다.

06 Many different communities around the world are currently engaged **[to / in]** language revitalization efforts.
현재 세계의 아주 많은 서로 다른 공동체들이 언어 재활성화 노력에 열중하고 있다.

DAY 30

Ⓐ 다음 빈칸에 알맞은 영어 단어나 우리말 뜻을 쓰시오.

01	content	① ______ ④ ______	② ______	③ ______
02	______	① 사각형 덩어리	② 구역, 블록	③ 막다, 방해하다
03	issue	① ______ ④ ______	② ______	③ ______
04	______	① 평평한, 수평의 ④ 심지어, ~조차	② 짝수의 ⑤ 훨씬	③ 공정한, 공평한
05	cover	① ______ ④ ______	② ______	③ ______
06	flat	① ______ ④ ______	② ______	③ ______
07	reason	① ______	② ______	③ ______
08	______	① 석방하다, 놓아주다, 석방, 해방 ③ 발표하다, 공개하다, 발표, 공개	② 방출하다, 방출 ④ 개봉하다, 출시하다, 개봉, 출시	
09	margin	① ______	② ______	③ ______
10	______	① 판, 칠판 ④ 하숙하다, 기숙사에 살다	② 이사회, 위원회	③ 탑승하다
11	______	① 주소	② 연설하다	③ 말하다
12	spring	① ______	② ______	③ ______

B 다음 영어 단어에 해당하는 우리말 뜻을 쓰시오.

01 phase	________	06 affect	________
02 phrase	________	07 effect	________
03 altitude	________	08 moral	________
04 aptitude	________	09 morale	________
05 attitude	________	10 mortal	________

C 다음 문장의 괄호 안에서 문맥상 알맞은 것을 고르시오.

01 The noise **[interrupted / interpreted]** anything and everything happening in the office.
그 소음은 사무실 안에서 발생하는 어떤 것이라도, 그리고 모든 것을 방해했다.

02 The government has to **[meditate / mediate]** the dispute between employers and employees.
정부는 고용주와 종업원 사이의 분쟁을 중재해야 한다.

03 We aim to conduct a **[competitive / comparative]** study of the educational systems of two countries.
우리는 두 나라의 교육 시스템에 대한 비교 연구를 수행하는 것을 목표로 한다.

04 They had to **[adapt / adopt]** quickly to the new environment.
그들은 새로운 환경에 재빨리 적응해야 했다.

05 When you don't sleep and have an **[access / excess]** of stress in your life, it shows in your skin.
당신이 잠을 자지 않고 삶에서 과도한 스트레스를 받을 때, 그것은 당신의 피부에 나타난다.

06 During the final stages of **[flight / fright]**, all passengers must remain seated.
비행의 마지막 단계 동안에는, 모든 승객이 좌석에 앉아 있어야 한다.

Word
∞ master

고등
BASIC

FINAL CHECK-UP

● 다음 영어 단어에 해당하는 우리말 뜻을 쓰시오.

01 complete	____________	21 belief	____________
02 distance	____________	22 combine	____________
03 period	____________	23 aim	____________
04 income	____________	24 certain	____________
05 moment	____________	25 damage	____________
06 reliable	____________	26 crime	____________
07 investigate	____________	27 quantity	____________
08 material	____________	28 situation	____________
09 fade	____________	29 due	____________
10 detail	____________	30 success	____________
11 improve	____________	31 found	____________
12 share	____________	32 emerge	____________
13 trait	____________	33 achieve	____________
14 discourage	____________	34 practical	____________
15 dedicate	____________	35 refuse	____________
16 increase	____________	36 express	____________
17 vital	____________	37 accept	____________
18 amaze	____________	38 expose	____________
19 separate	____________	39 resolution	____________
20 revise	____________	40 accomplish	____________

DAY 04~06

● 다음 영어 단어에 해당하는 우리말 뜻을 쓰시오.

01 infant	______	21 participation	______
02 impact	______	22 disappoint	______
03 category	______	23 opinion	______
04 effort	______	24 confuse	______
05 development	______	25 realistic	______
06 perspective	______	26 be aware of	______
07 discuss	______	27 locate	______
08 forecast	______	28 observe	______
09 progress	______	29 gather	______
10 trial	______	30 military	______
11 significant	______	31 forbid	______
12 provide A with B	______	32 exhibit	______
13 reward	______	33 exist	______
14 regular	______	34 invention	______
15 welfare	______	35 alarm	______
16 ancient	______	36 proper	______
17 pay attention to	______	37 except	______
18 handle	______	38 emission	______
19 determine	______	39 take on	______
20 efficient	______	40 conservative	______

다음 영어 단어에 해당하는 우리말 뜻을 쓰시오.

01 construct ____________
02 document ____________
03 precise ____________
04 transfer ____________
05 register ____________
06 grab ____________
07 comment ____________
08 sustainable ____________
09 application ____________
10 abandon ____________
11 define ____________
12 estimate ____________
13 glow ____________
14 aggressive ____________
15 appearance ____________
16 alternative ____________
17 firm ____________
18 reputation ____________
19 guarantee ____________
20 brilliant ____________
21 belong ____________
22 gender ____________
23 operation ____________
24 comfort ____________
25 behavior ____________
26 invest ____________
27 majority ____________
28 opposite ____________
29 remind A of B ____________
30 analyze ____________
31 declare ____________
32 vast ____________
33 barrier ____________
34 thrust ____________
35 education ____________
36 violent ____________
37 innocent ____________
38 submit ____________
39 incredible ____________
40 assign ____________

DAY 10~12

다음 영어 단어에 해당하는 우리말 뜻을 쓰시오.

01 consult	________	21 explicit	________
02 resemble	________	22 election	________
03 delicate	________	23 conversation	________
04 adversity	________	24 horizontal	________
05 temporary	________	25 inhabit	________
06 biological	________	26 identical	________
07 tremble	________	27 foster	________
08 restrict	________	28 adolescence	________
09 confront	________	29 destructive	________
10 vertical	________	30 rescue	________
11 disclose	________	31 negotiate	________
12 have difficulty (in) -ing	________	32 retire	________
13 implement	________	33 poverty	________
14 be related to	________	34 sacrifice	________
15 logical	________	35 apparent	________
16 carbon	________	36 length	________
17 asset	________	37 dominant	________
18 wire	________	38 remarkable	________
19 primitive	________	39 mutual	________
20 initial	________	40 hierarchy	________

● 다음 영어 단어에 해당하는 우리말 뜻을 쓰시오.

01 attendant ____________
02 irritate ____________
03 deprive ____________
04 diplomat ____________
05 urban ____________
06 imprison ____________
07 generous ____________
08 crawl ____________
09 justify ____________
10 adventure ____________
11 domestic ____________
12 hesitate ____________
13 offend ____________
14 suspect ____________
15 shift ____________
16 distribute ____________
17 refuge ____________
18 resident ____________
19 outcome ____________
20 arrogant ____________
21 strategy ____________
22 procedure ____________
23 privilege ____________
24 miracle ____________
25 faithful ____________
26 candidate ____________
27 promote ____________
28 dominate ____________
29 humiliate ____________
30 despair ____________
31 territory ____________
32 democracy ____________
33 tolerate ____________
34 shelter ____________
35 awkward ____________
36 eager ____________
37 genuine ____________
38 chief ____________
39 keep up with ____________
40 destination ____________

DAY 16 ~ 18

다음 영어 단어에 해당하는 우리말 뜻을 쓰시오.

01 contrast ______________

02 migrate ______________

03 flash ______________

04 mixture ______________

05 magical ______________

06 paradoxically ______________

07 be derived from ______________

08 conquer ______________

09 masterpiece ______________

10 gravity ______________

11 profound ______________

12 component ______________

13 nerve ______________

14 branch ______________

15 coordinate ______________

16 fiction ______________

17 series ______________

18 abstract ______________

19 collapse ______________

20 ritual ______________

21 tissue ______________

22 species ______________

23 orchestra ______________

24 impressive ______________

25 metaphor ______________

26 take ~ into account ______________

27 skeleton ______________

28 noble ______________

29 substance ______________

30 solid ______________

31 come up with ______________

32 outline ______________

33 encounter ______________

34 shallow ______________

35 ascend ______________

36 ultimate ______________

37 mammal ______________

38 humanity ______________

39 colonial ______________

40 architect ______________

DAY 19~21

다음 영어 단어에 해당하는 우리말 뜻을 쓰시오.

01 typical	______	21 isolate	______
02 install	______	22 transport	______
03 activate	______	23 commute	______
04 bleed	______	24 maximize	______
05 bother	______	25 physical	______
06 instruct	______	26 assist	______
07 result from	______	27 invade	______
08 chronic	______	28 have an effect on	______
09 fiber	______	29 recipe	______
10 explanation	______	30 accelerate	______
11 electronic	______	31 spare	______
12 admire	______	32 inevitable	______
13 symptom	______	33 edible	______
14 pupil	______	34 immune	______
15 diagnose	______	35 numerous	______
16 cure	______	36 collective	______
17 stroke	______	37 inspect	______
18 rough	______	38 posture	______
19 circuit	______	39 academic	______
20 voluntary	______	40 intellectual	______

DAY 22~24

다음 영어 단어에 해당하는 우리말 뜻을 쓰시오.

01 conserve ________

02 wasteful ________

03 diminish ________

04 frightened ________

05 rainforest ________

06 convert ________

07 dispose of ________

08 assumption ________

09 acid ________

10 fabric ________

11 attribute ________

12 interfere ________

13 commercial ________

14 innate ________

15 suitable ________

16 anxiety ________

17 purify ________

18 surface ________

19 transform ________

20 optimistic ________

21 respondent ________

22 endangered ________

23 desperate ________

24 remain ________

25 sweep ________

26 fragile ________

27 distraction ________

28 curiosity ________

29 end up -ing ________

30 cherish ________

31 evident ________

32 informative ________

33 sudden ________

34 pollution ________

35 viewer ________

36 stable ________

37 verbal ________

38 column ________

39 transmit ________

40 filter ________

● 다음 영어 단어에 해당하는 우리말 뜻을 쓰시오.

01 vain ______________
02 successive ______________
03 principle ______________
04 phenomenon ______________
05 intense ______________
06 wander ______________
07 sufficient ______________
08 curve ______________
09 principal ______________
10 defect ______________
11 flame ______________
12 native ______________
13 earthquake ______________
14 optional ______________
15 originate ______________
16 tropical ______________
17 respective ______________
18 barren ______________
19 literary ______________
20 considerable ______________
21 call off ______________
22 extinct ______________
23 frame ______________
24 literal ______________
25 imitate ______________
26 mess ______________
27 compliment ______________
28 absurd ______________
29 correct ______________
30 optimal ______________
31 float ______________
32 vogue ______________
33 agriculture ______________
34 freeze ______________
35 eruption ______________
36 instinct ______________
37 scared ______________
38 corporation ______________
39 feminine ______________
40 be known as ______________

DAY 28 ~ 30

● 다음 영어 단어에 해당하는 우리말 뜻을 쓰시오.

01 decline ____________

02 morale ____________

03 explore ____________

04 emergency ____________

05 terrific ____________

06 effect ____________

07 interrupt ____________

08 comparative ____________

09 fright ____________

10 precede ____________

11 meditate ____________

12 be concerned about ____________

13 statue ____________

14 hostility ____________

15 addiction ____________

16 ethnic ____________

17 circulate ____________

18 conscience ____________

19 personal ____________

20 moral ____________

21 status ____________

22 defend ____________

23 constant ____________

24 adopt ____________

25 altitude ____________

26 personnel ____________

27 terrible ____________

28 revolution ____________

29 mortal ____________

30 simulate ____________

31 be engaged in ____________

32 confirm ____________

33 calculate ____________

34 simultaneously ____________

35 council ____________

36 neural ____________

37 make up for ____________

38 counsel ____________

39 release ____________

40 figure ____________

Word
master

고등
BASIC

ANSWERS

DAILY CHECK-UP

DAY 01

A 01 포함하다 02 거절하다, 거부하다 03 ~을 실행[수행]하다, ~을 완료하다 04 공급하다, 제공하다, 대비하다 05 비슷한, 유사한 06 사라지다, 없어지다 07 증가하다, 증가시키다, 증가, 인상 08 뛰어난, 우월한, 상급의, 윗사람, 상급자 09 믿음, 신념, 신앙 10 공급하다, 제공하다, 공급 11 순간, 중요성 12 거절하다, 거부하다 13 개선하다, 향상하다 14 열등한, 하위의, 손아랫사람, 하급자 15 나타나다, 모습을 드러내다, (생각·사실 등이) 드러나다 16 생산하다, 만들어 내다, 초래하다, 농산물 17 실용적인, 실제적인 18 희미해지다, 사라지다 19 나누다, 공유하다, 몫 20 (깊은) 슬픔, 비탄

B 01 indifferent 02 common 03 emotion 04 advanced 05 recover 06 seek 07 run into 08 experience 09 aim 10 consider 11 success 12 depend on[upon] 13 certain 14 decrease 15 slight 16 quantity 17 situation 18 failure 19 express 20 accept

C 01 enhance 02 amount 03 pursue / search 04 inferior 05 accept 06 feeling / sentiment 07 rare 08 exclude 09 location / context 10 perform / complete

D 01 similar 02 increased 03 advanced 04 indifferent 05 faded 06 practical

DAY 02

A 01 설립하다, 기초를 세우다 02 이루다, 성취하다 03 노출시키다, 폭로하다 04 믿을 수 있는, 의지가 되는 05 결합[연합]하다, 결속시키다 06 빠른 07 아주 중요한, 필수적인, 생명 유지에 필요한 08 이루다, 성취하다 09 극복하다, 이기다, 압도하다 10 범죄, 범행, 죄악 11 불법적인, 위법인 12 장기, 기관 13 분리하다, 별개의, 각각의 14 ~으로 이어지다, ~을 야기[초래]하다 15 설립하다, 확립하다, 수립하다 16 ~을 받을 만하다, ~할 가치가 있다 17 기간, 시기, 시대 18 드러내다, 폭로하다 19 잘못 인도하다, 오해하게 하다 20 결합시키다, 겸비하다

B 01 get along with 02 recognize 03 chase 04 amount 05 connect 06 deal with 07 conceal 08 process 09 devote 10 perceive 11 continue 12 local 13 random 14 historical 15 expert 16 dedicate 17 complete 18 exhausted 19 decade 20 charity

C 01 total 02 recognize 03 cease 04 worn out 05 conceal 06 separate 07 accomplish 08 essential / significant 09 cause 10 planned

D 01 reliable 02 deserve 03 rapid 04 dedicate 05 exposed 06 deal with

DAY 03

A 01 이익, 혜택, 자선 행사, 이롭다, 이익을 얻다 02 거리, 간격 03 포함하다, 억누르다 04 의학의, 의료의 05 있을 법한, 예상되는 06 연구[조사]하다, 연구, 조사 07 재료, 자료, 물질, 물질의, 육체적인 08 다양한, 여러 가지의 09 공식적인, 공무의, 정식의 10 용기를 북돋우다, 격려하다, 장려하다 11 특성, 특색 12 포함[수반]하다, 관련시키다 13 집중하다, 전력을 기울이다 14 수입, 소득 15 표시하다, 채점하다, 표시, 흔적 16 조사하다, 연구하다 17 만기가 된, ~을 하기로 되어 있는 18 이익, 수익, 이윤, 이익을 얻다 19 추구하다, 추적하다 20 부정적인, 음성의

B 01 alter 02 according to 03 direct 04 detail 05 contact 06 examine 07 participate in 08 resolution 09 search 10 performance 11 diverse 12 knowledge 13 revise 14 discourage 15 disturb 16 opportunity 17 ignore 18 damage 19 amaze 20 look into

C 01 damage 02 disregard / neglect 03 diverse 04 exclude 05 substance 06 take part in 07 disturb / distract 08 positive 09 feature / property 10 expenditure

D 01 encouraged 02 marked 03 official 04 amaze 05 contain 06 investigate

DAY 04

A 01 환경, 상황, 형편 02 발전, 성장, 개발 03 영향(력), 영향을 주다 04 발생하다, 일어나다, 생각나다 05 예측하다, 예보하다, 예측, 예보 06 열정, 격정 07 전체의, 완전한 08 강조[역설]하다, 두드러지게 하다 09 허락[허용]하다 10 즉각적인, 직접의 11 (자연·주변의) 환경 12 참가, 참여 13 유지하다, 지지하다, 부양하다 14 보수적인, 보수주의의 15 금지하다 16 영향, 충격, 영향[충격]을 주다 17 배출, 방출, 배출물 18 측정하다, 재다, 측정, 조치 19 예측하다, 예언하다 20 존경[존중]하다, 존경, 측면

B 01 prevent 02 support 03 effort 04 progress 05 due to 06 perspective 07 necessity 08 tendency 09 preference 10 concern 11 be aware of 12 significant 13 active 14 community 15 provide A with B 16 regular 17 ancient 18 determine 19 military 20 function

C 01 enthusiasm 02 partial 03 circumstance 04 prohibit 05 passive 06 influence / affect 07 irregular 08 support 09 modern 10 instant

D 01 preference 02 significant 03 provide, with 04 concern 05 function 06 emphasized

DAY 05

A 01 주장하다, 요구하다, 주장, 요구, 청구 02 가정하다, 추정하다 03 접근하다, 접근 04 ~을 가리키다, ~을 언급하다, ~을 참고하다 05 모이다, 모으다 06 조직하다, 준비하다, 정리하다 07 존재하다, (근근이) 살아가다 08 정리[배열]하다, 준비하다 09 결정적인, 중대한 10 측면, 양상, 관점 11 목적, 의도, 결심 12 묘사하다, 설명하다 13 동기를 부여하다, 자극하다 14 혼동하다, 혼란시키다 15 대표하다, 나타내다, 대변하다 16 전시하다, 보이다, 전시품 17 (주의·관심 등을) 끌다, 끌어들이다, 매혹하다 18 조정하다, 조절하다 19 치료(법), 대우, 처리 20 전시하다, 드러내다, 전시

B 01 purchase 02 disappoint 03 accident 04 demand 05 general 06 alarm 07 fee 08 specific 09 reward 10 take on 11 communicate 12 compare 13 disorder 14 manage 15 handle 16 universal 17 pay attention to 18 apologize 19 observe 20 recommend

C 01 chaos 02 assume 03 arrange 04 satisfy 05 depict / portray 06 discourage 07 manage 08 undertake / employ 09 supply 10 critical

D 01 disorder 02 aspects 03 communicate 04 attract 05 exhibit 06 specific

DAY 06

A 01 토론하다, 논의하다 02 불평[항의]하다, 호소하다 03 적절한, 적합한 04 주요한, 최초의, 초등의, 근본적인 05 범주, 부문 06 복지, 행복 07 분투하다, 애쓰다, 싸움, 노력 08 적절한, 올바른 09 독, 독약, 독을 넣다, 해치다 10 두다, ~의 위치를 알아내다 11 반응하다, 응답하다 12 발명, 발명품, 날조 13 토론[논의]하다, 숙고하다, 토론, 논쟁 14 ~을 제외하고, 제외하다 15 개념, 생각 16 결론을 내리다, 끝내다 17 표준, 기준, 규범 18 나타내다, 가리키다, 암시하다 19 대체[대신]하다, 교체하다 20 필수의, 중요한, 본질적인

B 01 trial 02 unique 03 can afford to *do* 04 advertise 05 realistic 06 supplement 07 chemical 08 judgment 09 credit 10 eliminate 11 standard 12 efficient 13 ideal 14 infant 15 opinion 16 consume 17 run out of 18 awareness 19 alive 20 valuable

C 01 produce 02 standard 03 inefficient 04 debate 05 strive 06 ordinary 07 major / essential 08 preserve 09 notion 10 realistic

D 01 valuable 02 advertised 03 complain 04 indicates 05 located 06 running out of

DAILY CHECK-UP

DAY 07

A 01 고용하다, 이용하다 02 훌륭한, 뛰어난, 눈부신 03 요인, 요소 04 항의하다, 주장하다, 항의, 시위 05 장벽, 장애물, 한계 06 임명[지명]하다, (시간·장소 등을) 정하다 07 거대한, 막대한 08 고용하다 09 치명적인, 극도의, 죽은 듯이, 극도로 10 투자하다, (시간·노력 등을) 쏟다 11 평균, 표준, 평균의 12 지원, 신청(서), 적용 13 출판[발행]하다, 발표하다 14 장애(물) 15 재정, 재무, 자금, 자금을 대다 16 정의하다, 규정하다 17 요소, 성분, 원소, 원리 18 평범한, 보통의 19 합리적인, 분별 있는, (가격이) 적정한 20 거대한, 방대한

B 01 occasion 02 blend 03 get used to 04 education 05 donate 06 alternative 07 firm 08 interest 09 appearance 10 organic 11 worth 12 gender 13 independence 14 rare 15 previous 16 abandon 17 incredible 18 detect 19 figure out 20 tiny

C 01 unbelievable 02 hire 03 subsequent 04 outstanding 05 fatal 06 tiny 07 rational 08 extraordinary 09 designate / nominate 10 solid

D 01 organic 02 rare 03 alternative 04 define 05 detected 06 independence

DAY 08

A 01 만족(감) 02 (대)다수, 대부분 03 편안함, 위로, 편하게 하다, 위로하다 04 편안함, 용이함, 편하게 하다, 덜어 주다 05 (~을) 할 수 있게 하다, 가능하게 하다 06 보존하다, 지키다, 저장하다 07 문서, 서류, 기록하다 08 경향, 추세, 유행 09 감염, 전염 10 붙잡다, 움켜잡다, 움켜잡음 11 가족, 가정, 가족[가정]의 12 보험 13 경제의, 경제학의 14 기념하다, 축하하다, 찬양하다 15 문장, 판결, 선고, 판결을 내리다, 형을 선고하다 16 정확한, 정밀한 17 달아나다, 탈출하다, 탈출, 도망 18 정확한, 정밀한, 꼼꼼한 19 경쟁하다, 겨루다 20 ~보다는, ~ 대신에, ~하지 말고

B 01 refreshing 02 journal 03 vehicle 04 private 05 operation 06 belong 07 opposite 08 transfer 09 submit 10 innovate 11 blame 12 theory 13 estimate 14 demonstrate 15 disaster 16 insight 17 assign 18 dozens of 19 avoid 20 motion

C 01 ease 02 contentment 03 minority 04 grasp / seize 05 accuse 06 reverse 07 flee 08 allocate / designate 09 inaccurate 10 surrender

D 01 estimate 02 innovate 03 enable 04 transferring 05 demonstrated 06 preserved

DAY 09

A 01 심각한, 엄격한 02 보증하다, 보증, 담보 03 폭력적인, 격렬한, 심한 04 (처)벌하다, 응징하다 05 위기 06 기억해 내다, 상기시키다, 회수하다, 회상, 회수 07 적당한, 충분한, 적임인 08 분석하다 09 미루다, 연기하다, 지체하게 하다, 지연, 연기 10 유전적인, 유전학의 11 논평, 언급, 의견, 논평하다, 의견을 말하다 12 대리인, 중개인, (공공 기관의) 직원 13 공격적인, 매우 적극적인, 침략적인 14 회전하다, 교대로 하다, 자전하다 15 해결하다, 정착하다, 안정시키다 16 빛나다, 타다, 상기되다, 불빛, 홍조 17 천재성, 천재 18 등록하다, 기록하다, 등록 19 인정하다 20 문명

B 01 be based on 02 commit 03 construct 04 load 05 mature 06 declare 07 manufacture 08 edit 09 thrust 10 remind A of B 11 equip 12 gradually 13 corporate 14 deny 15 alert 16 sustainable 17 behavior 18 innocent 19 guilty 20 reputation

C 01 announce 02 remark 03 burden 04 praise 05 fame / prestige 06 rapidly / radically 07 shine 08 destroy / demolish 09 appropriate 10 innocent

D 01 civilizations 02 registered 03 settle 04 aggressive 05 guarantee 06 matures

DAY 10

A 01 명백한, 분명한 02 소유하다, 지니다, 사로잡다 03 조심스러운, 신중한 04 조상, 선조 05 떨다, 흔들리다, 걱정하다, 떨림 06 길이, 시간 07 영구적인, 영원한 08 분명한, 외관상의 09 희생, 희생자 10 넓어지다, 넓히다 11 운동선수 12 논리적인, 타당한 13 자격 있는, 적임의 14 전기 15 고집하다, 지속되다 16 출발, 출항 17 물려받다, 이어받다, 상속받다 18 끌다, 끌리다, 끌기, 장애물 19 넓히다, 연장하다, 뻗다 20 ~에 기여하다, ~의 원인이 되다

B 01 be related to 02 vertical 03 remarkable 04 retire 05 resist 06 temporary 07 devise 08 restrict 09 horizontal 10 reform 11 sacrifice 12 individual 13 regulate 14 clarify 15 memorize 16 aboard 17 initial 18 embrace 19 delicate 20 rescue

C 01 apparent 02 permanent 03 shiver 04 vertical 05 reject 06 extend 07 arrival 08 control / adjust 09 offspring / descendant 10 limit

D 01 cautious 02 remarkable 03 sacrifices 04 inherit 05 initial 06 delicate

DAY 11

A 01 양육하다, 육성하다, 촉진하다 02 인구, 주민, 개체군 03 (요리의) 재료, 성분, 구성 요소 04 (흩)뿌리다, 흩어지다[흩어지게 하다] 05 ~을 겪다, ~을 거치다, ~을 조사하다 06 나누다[나뉘다], 분열되다, 갈라지다 07 다수의, 많은, 복합적인 08 마찰, 갈등 09 양육하다, 육성하다, 양육, 교육 10 상처를 입히다, 감정을 상하게 하다, 상처, 부상 11 원인이 되다, 야기[초래]하다, 원인 12 용량, 수용력, 능력 13 추적하다, 추적하여 찾아내다, 자취, 흔적 14 밝히다, 폭로하다, 드러내다 15 능력, 재능 16 발견하다, 알아내다, 발굴하다 17 거대한, 대량의 18 협상[교섭]하다, 타결하다 19 갈등, 충돌, 충돌[대립]하다 20 고발하다, 비난하다

B 01 have difficulty (in) -ing 02 pressure 03 election 04 consequence 05 outstanding 06 be regarded as 07 wire 08 conversation 09 adversity 10 exotic 11 biological 12 carbon 13 analogy 14 professional 15 cognitive 16 available 17 reference 18 restore 19 asset 20 intelligent

C 01 discourse 02 effect / consequence 03 nurture 04 track 05 capacity 06 reconstruct 07 assemble 08 tiny 09 numerous 10 property

D 01 available 02 accused 03 analogy 04 cognitive 05 adversity 06 Exotic

DAY 12

A 01 현대의, 현대인 02 단점, 결점, 장애 03 파괴적인 04 가능성, 실현성, 장래성 05 꾸준한, 한결같은 06 널리 퍼진, 광범위한 07 닮다, 유사하다 08 맞서다, 직면하게 만들다 09 강화하다, 증강하다, 보강하다 10 잠재적인, 가능성 있는, 잠재력, 가능성 11 장식하다, 꾸미다 12 동시대의, 현대의, 당대의, 동시대인 13 단점, 약점, 불이익 14 전문 지식[기술] 15 청소년기 16 통합하다, 통합되다 17 강화하다, 견고히 하다 18 이행하다, 실행하다, 도구 19 동일한, 일치하는 20 ~을 야기[초래]하다, ~을 유발하다

B 01 hierarchy 02 industrial 03 frequency 04 primitive 05 consult 06 dominant 07 relevant 08 attach 09 mutual 10 poverty 11 in terms of 12 enthusiastic 13 urgent 14 explicit 15 wealth 16 fundamental 17 classify 18 reproduce 19 approve 20 inhabit

C 01 implicit 02 dwell / reside 03 constant 04 poverty 05 take after 06 reciprocal 07 weaken 08 categorize 09 passionate 10 subordinate

D 01 contemporary 02 relevant 03 integrated 04 Hierarchy 05 frequency 06 implement

DAILY CHECK-UP

DAY 13

A 01 힐긋[얼핏] 보다, 힐긋 봄 02 화를 내다, 분개하다 03 터무니없는, 어리석은, 우스운 04 충실한 05 진실된, 진심의 06 충동 07 책임감 있는, 책임이 있는 08 창피를 주다, 굴욕감을 느끼게 하다 09 참을 수 없는, 성급한 10 진짜의, 진실한 11 짜증나게[화나게] 하다, 거슬리다 12 참다, 견디다, 용인하다 13 질투하는 14 주저하다, 망설이다 15 좌절감을 느끼는 16 절망, 절망하다 17 자신감 있는, 확신하는 18 견디다, 참다 19 우울(증), 불황 20 열망하는, 열심인

B 01 frank 02 awkward 03 miserable 04 arouse 05 ashamed 06 applause 07 fascinated 08 compassion 09 astonished 10 crawl 11 delight 12 anticipate 13 generous 14 humble 15 arrogant 16 offend 17 empathy 18 put up with 19 make sense of 20 reluctant

C 01 genuine 02 glimpse 03 humble / modest 04 tolerate / endure / bear 05 insult 06 willing 07 awaken 08 expect 09 irresponsible 10 sympathy

D 01 make sense of 02 depression 03 irritate 04 empathy 05 ridiculous 06 faithful

DAY 14

A 01 협력하다 02 절차, 수순 03 유대, 결속, 채권 04 전략 05 인출하다, 철회하다 06 동기, 유인, 장려(책) 07 허드렛일, 집안일 08 직업, 점유 09 안전한, 안정된, 안전하게 하다 10 일과, 늘 하던 방식, 일상적인 11 (단체의) 장(長), 우두머리, 주요한, 최고의 12 종업원, 수행원 13 바꾸다, 이동하다, 변화, 이동, 교대 14 박탈하다, 빼앗다 15 도전, 난관, 도전하다 16 전문적으로 하다, 전공하다 17 익숙한, 친숙한, 잘 아는 18 시골의 19 긴장, 부담, 긴장시키다, 혹사하다 20 기적

B 01 supervise 02 accompany 03 exchange 04 outcome 05 adventure 06 react 07 colleague 08 keep up with 09 resident 10 urban 11 remote 12 negotiation 13 make the most of 14 certificate 15 companion 16 shelter 17 deposit 18 exceed 19 destination 20 complicated

C 01 direct 02 deposit 03 intimate 04 trade 05 rural 06 distant / isolated 07 complex 08 insecure 09 rob 10 dweller

D 01 specialize 02 collaborate 03 negotiation 04 keeping up with 05 strategy 06 destination

DAY 15

A 01 지배하다, 우세하다 02 환불, 환불하다 03 국내의, 가정의 04 금지하다, 금지 05 고소하다, 소송을 제기하다 06 투옥하다, 감금하다 07 산업화하다 08 기금, 자금, 자금을 대다 09 (입국) 이민, 이주 10 수수료, 위원회 11 빛지다, 신세지다 12 통치하다, 지배[좌우]하다 13 재산, 특성 14 외교관 15 위반하다, 침해하다 16 중역, 간부, 경영진, 중역의, 실행하는 17 특권, 특혜, 특권을 주다 18 의심하다, 용의자 19 권위, 당국 20 민주주의, 민주국가

B 01 refuge 02 in charge of 03 regardless of 04 distribute 05 compromise 06 justify 07 dispute 08 territory 09 debt 10 witness 11 equivalent 12 radical 13 patent 14 region 15 administration 16 priority 17 candidate 18 commodity 19 promote 20 wield

C 01 emigration 02 govern 03 argue 04 foreign 05 disobey / invade 06 asset 07 gradual 08 merchandise 09 forbid 10 permit

D 01 territory 02 executives 03 authority 04 equivalents 05 priority 06 distribute

DAY 16

A 01 액체, 액체의, 유동체의 02 화산의, 화산 작용에 의한 03 유기체, 생물 04 해골, 뼈대 05 종(種), 종류 06 천문학 07 온도, 기온, 체온 08 증기, 수증기, 증발하다 09 조직, 화장지 10 포식자, 약탈자 11 혼합, 혼합물 12 입자, 극소량 13 이주하다, (새·동물이) 이동하다 14 포유동물 15 중력, 중대성 16 줄기, 유래하다 17 추출하다, 뽑아내다, 추출물 18 폭발하다, 터뜨리다, 파열 19 층, 층층이 쌓다 20 유체, 유동체, 유동체의

B 01 hypothesis 02 habitat 03 branch 04 metal 05 come up with 06 laboratory 07 survive 08 gas 09 glacier 10 consist of 11 ray 12 keep A from -ing 13 method 14 vibrate 15 solid 16 component 17 nerve 18 molecule 19 observation 20 toxic

C 01 explode / go off 02 liquid 03 prey 04 creature 05 bough 06 beam 07 be composed[comprised] of / be made (up) of 08 ingredient

D 01 laboratory 02 toxic 03 particle 04 molecules 05 vibrate 06 coming up with

DAY 17

A 01 편견, 편견을 갖게 하다 02 정신, 영혼 03 오르다, 올라가다 04 비극의, 비참한 05 (글의) 맥락, (사건의) 정황 06 희극의, 웃기는 07 심오한, 깊은 08 신화, (근거 없는) 사회적 통념 09 역설적으로 10 윤곽을 그리다, 개요를 말하다, 개요, 윤곽 11 수정하다, 변형하다 12 얕은, 피상적인, 천박한 13 식민지의 14 줄거리, 음모, 음모를 꾸미다 15 편견, 편향, 편견[선입견]을 갖게 하다 16 인류, 인간성, 인간애 17 절대적인, 완전한 18 반대하다, 방해하다, 대항하다 19 귀족의, 고귀한, 귀족 20 반어적으로, 역설적으로

B 01 substance 02 philosophy 03 spell 04 metaphor 05 draft 06 take ~ into account 07 simplify 08 empower 09 ultimate 10 heritage 11 imply 12 artificial 13 ritual 14 conquer 15 series 16 inherent 17 conventional 18 translate 19 be derived from 20 fiction

C 01 legacy 02 profound 03 ceremony 04 traditional 05 complicate 06 analogy 07 authorize 08 paradoxically 09 tragic 10 intrinsic

D 01 artificial 02 translate 03 colonial 04 derived from 05 biases 06 contexts

DAY 18

A 01 초상화 02 추상적인, 개요, 추출하다, 요약하다 03 즐겁게 하다 04 정교한, 공들인 05 조정하다, 동등한 06 조화를 이루다, 화음을 넣다 07 주제, 테마 08 진짜의, 진본[진품]인 09 창의적인 10 오케스트라, 관현악단 11 외부의 12 인기 13 인상적인, 감동적인 14 입장, 입구, 입학 15 연구소, 협회, 설립하다 16 연습[시연]하다, 리허설을 하다 17 상상력이 풍부한, 상상의 18 즐겁게 하다 19 (우연히) 만나다 20 번쩍이다, 번쩍임, 플래시

B 01 architect 02 masterpiece 03 classical 04 perform 05 craft 06 distinguish 07 compose 08 concrete 09 precious 10 memorial 11 internal 12 differ 13 polish 14 contrast 15 magical 16 collapse 17 proportion 18 socialize 19 play a role (in) 20 be associated with

C 01 entertain 02 exit 03 monument 04 concrete 05 valuable 06 striking 07 external 08 differentiate

D 01 creative 02 elaborate 03 authentic 04 coordinate 05 imaginative 06 proportion

DAILY CHECK-UP

DAY 19

A 01 최소화하다 02 곱하다, 크게 증가시키다 03 통근하다, 통근, 통근 거리[시간] 04 설치하다, 설비하다 05 서두르다, 돌진하다 06 자동의, 무의식적인 07 승객 08 수송하다, 운반하다, 수송 09 시각의, 눈에 보이는, 시각 자료 10 방정식 11 종류, 부류, 분류하다 12 풀다, 느슨하게 하다 13 (세밀히) 조사하다 14 추락하다, 충돌하다, 추락, 충돌 15 가상의, 사실상의 16 각도 17 충전하다, 재충전하다 18 전자의 19 항해하다, 조종하다, 길을 찾다 20 여분의, 예비의, 할애하다, 아끼다

B 01 statistics 02 download 03 aircraft 04 bump 05 rough 06 activate 07 assemble 08 shipment 09 ride 10 numerous 11 upload 12 mechanical 13 astronaut 14 accelerate 15 manual 16 nuclear 17 maximize 18 circuit 19 have A in common 20 turn A into B

C 01 uneven / approximate 02 set up 03 download 04 countless 05 minimize 06 extra 07 automatic 08 classify 09 investigate 10 tighten

D 01 virtual 02 astronaut 03 navigate 04 activate 05 mechanical 06 turned, into

DAY 20

A 01 치료하다, 고치다, 치유(법) 02 (경기용) 트랙, 자국, 추적하다 03 (팔다리 등을) 뻗다, 늘리다, 뻗기, 스트레칭, 신축성 04 치료, 요법 05 타격, 뇌졸중 06 피로 07 피를 흘리다, 출혈하다 08 향기, 냄새 09 휘젓다, 자극하다, 휘젓기, 동요 10 자세, 자세를 취하다 11 조리법, 비법, 비결 12 치료하다, 치유되다 13 줄, 열, 노를 젓다 14 증상, 징후 15 쏟다, 흘리다, 유출 16 영양소, 영양분 17 ~으로 고통받다, ~을 앓다 18 일부, 1인분, 분배하다 19 임신한 20 구부릴 수 있는, 유연한, 융통성 있는

B 01 prescribe 02 surgery 03 breath 04 fiber 05 immune 06 edible 07 starve 08 digestion 09 faint 10 muscle 11 extreme 12 flavor 13 chronic 14 diagnose 15 opponent 16 have an effect on 17 target 18 dietary 19 physical 20 obesity

C 01 taste 02 heal 03 mental 04 pass out 05 inedible 06 competitor 07 acute / temporary 08 aim

D 01 postures 02 extreme 03 immune 04 suffered from 05 nutrients 06 Dietary

DAY 21

A 01 평가하다 02 전형적인, 보통의 03 자발적인, 자원봉사의 04 수여하다, 인정하다, 보조금 05 정책, 방침 06 존경하다, 감탄하다 07 주장하다, 논쟁하다 08 중간의, 중급의 09 지도, 안내 10 지적인, 지성의, 지식인 11 돕다, 조력 12 침략하다, 침입하다 13 피할 수 없는, 당연한 14 학생, 눈동자 15 학업의, 학구적인 16 훈육하다, 규율, 훈육, 학과 17 돕다, 조력하다, 지원, 도움 18 수여하다, 상, 상금 19 평가하다, 산정하다 20 엄격한

B 01 score 02 result from 03 presentation 04 instruct 05 gratitude 06 isolate 07 formal 08 bother 09 collective 10 disguise 11 enroll 12 command 13 recruit 14 get rid of 15 trigger 16 range 17 captive 18 interact 19 explanation 20 attempt

C 01 gather / assemble 02 inescapable / unavoidable 03 award 04 individual 05 eliminate 06 excuse / interpretation 07 disturb 08 informal 09 assess / estimate 10 aid

D 01 gratitude 02 intellectual 03 interact 04 invade 05 intermediate 06 disciplined

DAY 22

A 01 깜짝 놀란, 겁먹은 02 설득하다, 확신시키다 03 심리, 심리학 04 안도, 구조, 완화 05 안정된, 견고한 06 간섭하다, 방해하다 07 타고난, 선천적인, 고유의 08 호기심 09 설득하다 10 ~의 탓[덕분]으로 돌리다, 속성, 자질 11 ~할 작정이다, 의도하다 12 가정, 추측, 인수 13 갑작스러운 14 간섭하다, 개입하다, 중재하다 15 압도하다, 사로잡다 16 연상하다, 연관 짓다, 동료 17 두려워하는 18 속이다, 부정행위를 하다 19 스트레스, 강조, 강조하다, 압박하다 20 호의적인, 우호적인

B 01 desperate 02 illusion 03 ignorant 04 anxiety 05 uneasy 06 end up -ing 07 identify 08 distraction 09 optimistic 10 skeptical 11 out of place 12 subjective 13 burden 14 exclude 15 undergo 16 ensure 17 complex 18 mental 19 boost 20 manipulate

C 01 convince 02 objective 03 inborn 04 ascribe 05 simple 06 intervene 07 worry / concern 08 hostile 09 abrupt 10 include

D 01 manipulating 02 identified 03 desperate 04 overwhelmed 05 distraction 06 skeptical

DAY 23

A 01 발표하다, 알리다 02 감소하다, 약화시키다 03 높이다, 향상시키다 04 누설하다, 새다, 새는 곳, 누출 05 더미, 쌓아 놓은 것, 쌓다 06 시청자, 관객 07 방송하다, 널리 알리다 08 간결한, 잠시의, 짧은 보고, 요약하다 09 거래, 매매, 처리(과정) 10 휴대용의, 이동이 쉬운 11 배달하다, 연설하다, 분만하다 12 청중, 관중, 시청자 13 변수, 변하기 쉬운 14 줄다, 완화시키다 15 움직이기 쉬운, 기동성의 16 말의, 언어의, 구두의 17 매력적인, 흥미를 끄는 18 매체, 수단, 방법, 중간의 19 (눈에) 보이는 20 (인공)위성

B 01 column 02 limitation 03 commercial 04 evident 05 obscure 06 informative 07 respondent 08 feel free to *do* 09 illustrate 10 compelling 11 affair 12 signal 13 envelope 14 union 15 get in touch with 16 stamp 17 collect 18 wrap 19 transmit 20 convey

C 01 improve / increase 02 audience 03 alliance 04 attractive 05 obscure 06 communicate / transport 07 invisible 08 instructive 09 stationary 10 restriction

D 01 verbal 02 transmits 03 commercials 04 compelling 05 satellite 06 variables

DAY 24

A 01 멸종 위기에 처한, 위험에 빠진 02 전환하다, 바꾸다 03 활용하다, 이용하다 04 버리다, 폐기하다 05 경사, 경사지다, (마음이) 기울다 06 부서지기 쉬운, 취약한 07 낭비하는, 헛된 08 가파른, 급격한 09 보존[보호]하다, 아끼다 10 남아 있다, 여전히 ~인 채로 있다 11 화석 12 산봉우리, 정상, 정점, 절정에 이르다 13 빨대, 짚, 지푸라기 14 변형시키다, 바꾸다 15 ~을 버리다, ~을 처리하다[없애다] 16 발생시키다, 만들어 내다 17 날것의, 가공하지 않은 18 대기(권), 분위기 19 산(酸), 산성의 20 깨끗이 하다, 정화하다

B 01 surface 02 resource 03 filter 04 landscape 05 suitable 06 rainforest 07 litter 08 pesticide 09 recycle 10 landfill 11 cliff 12 reduce 13 (the) chances are (that) 14 accumulate 15 threaten 16 ecosystem 17 sweep 18 cherish 19 fabric 20 pollution

C 01 processed 02 appropriate 03 garbage / waste 04 exterior / emerge 05 endanger 06 decline 07 scenery 08 transform 09 contamination 10 pollute / contaminate

D 01 dispose of 02 fragile 03 conserve 04 accumulate 05 atmosphere 06 ecosystems

DAILY CHECK-UP

DAY 25

A 01 물을 빼내다, 배수하다, 소모시키다, 배수관, 소모 02 기후 03 부화하다 04 녹다, 녹이다 05 농업 06 ~을 차지하다, ~을 인계받다, ~을 인수하다 07 뜨다, 떠다니다 08 경작하다, (작물을) 재배하다, 기르다 09 사나운, 극심한 10 (기후가) 온화한, (행동이) 차분한 11 비옥하게 하다, 풍요롭게 하다 12 수확하다, 수확, 수확물 13 그림자, 그늘, 그늘지게 하다 14 내구성이 있는 15 가뭄 16 농작물, 수확물 17 비옥한, 번식력이 있는 18 가벼운, 밝은, 밝히다, 빛 19 민속의, 민간의, 사람들 20 극심한, 치열한

B 01 take advantage of 02 native 03 tropical 04 phenomenon 05 creature 06 originate 07 humid 08 ripe 09 freeze 10 pest 11 annual 12 sufficient 13 barren 14 earthquake 15 eruption 16 resistant 17 tide 18 wave 19 weed 20 transplant

C 01 fierce / extreme / severe 02 fertile 03 melt 04 adequate 05 derive 06 sink 07 mild 08 plow 09 delicate / fragile 10 reap

D 01 humid 02 resistant 03 tropical 04 annual 05 eruptions 06 phenomenon

DAY 26

A 01 develop 02 ① 공기 ② 공중 ③ 항공 ④ 방송하다 03 check 04 ① 존경, 존중 ② 관련 ③ 안부 ④ ~으로 간주하다[여기다] 05 ① 내다, 산출하다, 산출량 ② 양도하다 ③ 굴복하다 06 object 07 still 08 ① 관습, 풍습 ② 관세, 세관 ③ 맞춘, 주문 제작한 09 ① 예금, 은행 계좌 ② 이유, 근거 ③ 설명하다, 해명하다, 책임지다, 설명, 이야기 ④ 차지하다 10 correct 11 tip 12 ① 요금을 청구하다, 요금 ② (일을) 맡기다, 책임, 담당 ③ 비난하다, 고발하다, 혐의, 고발 ④ 충전하다, 채우다, 충전

B 01 덩어리, 집단, 부피, 질량, 대량의, 대중의 02 엉망, 혼란한 상태, 더럽히다 03 문자 그대로의, 문자(상)의 04 읽고 쓸 수 있는 05 문학의, 문학적인 06 인용하다 07 장소, 위치, 현장 08 시각적인, 광학의 09 선택적인 10 최적의, 최상의

C 01 sacred 02 expends 03 extinct 04 considerable 05 famine 06 for

DAY 27

A 01 ① 계약서, 계약, 계약하다 ② 수축하다, 줄어들다 ③ (병에) 걸리다 02 sound 03 ① 청구서, 계산서 ② 지폐 ③ 법안 ④ (새의) 부리 04 ① 성격 ② 특징 ③ 등장인물 ④ 글자 05 bear 06 balance 07 subject 08 ① 세다, 계산하다, 셈, 계산, 총계 ② 중요하다 ③ 간주하다[여기다] 09 draw 10 ① 무덤, 묘 ② 심각한 ③ 중대한, 중요한 11 ① 현재의, 현재 ② 있는, 존재하는, 출석한 ③ 선물 ④ 제시하다, (보여) 주다, 발표하다 12 hold

B 01 교장, 우두머리, 주요한, 중요한 02 원칙, 원리, 신념 03 패배시키다, 패배 04 결함, 결점 05 뼈대, 틀, 액자 06 불길, 불꽃 07 조각하다, 새기다 08 곡선, 커브 09 흡수하다 10 터무니없는, 불합리한

C 01 complement 02 initiated 03 respective 04 successive 05 defects 06 cooperation

DAY 28

A 01 ① 벌금, 벌금을 부과하다 ② 훌륭한, 좋은 ③ 고운, 미세한 ④ (날씨가) 맑은[좋은] 02 ① 현재의 ② 흐름 ③ 경향, 추세 ④ 전류 03 term 04 ① 해결, 해결책 ② 용액 05 book 06 ① 비율 ② 속도 ③ 요금 ④ 평가하다 07 fair 08 conduct 09 ① 비판적인 ② 중요한, 중대한 ③ 결정적인, 위기의 10 press 11 ① 특징, ~을 특징으로 하다 ② 이목구비 ③ 특집 기사[방송] 12 ① 상태 ② 환경, 상황 ③ 조건, 조항

B 01 양심 02 의식하는, 의식이 있는, 의도적인 03 비상사태 04 출현, 발생 05 올리다, 들어올리다 06 오르다, 올라가다 07 개인적인 08 인원, 직원, 인사과 09 의존하다 10 방어[수비]하다, 변호하다

C 01 evolution 02 simulate 03 conform 04 neural 05 calculates 06 with

DAY 29

A 01 decline 02 ① 정장 ② 소송 ③ 맞다, 어울리다 03 ① 일치하다 ② 해당[상응]하다 ③ 서신을 주고받다 ④ 조화를 이루다 04 dismiss 05 post 06 ① 경우, 사례 ② 사건, 문제 ③ 소송 ④ 상자, 용기 07 ① 기사 ② 물건, 물품 ③ 조항, 조건 08 reserve 09 company 10 ① 반사하다 ② 반영하다 ③ 심사숙고하다, 회고하다 11 ① 진가를 알아보다, (제대로) 이해하다 ② 감사하다, 고마워하다 ③ 감상하다 12 figure

B 01 상태, 국가, 말하다, 진술하다 02 조각상 03 지위, 신분, 상황 04 허리 05 낭비, 폐기물, 낭비하다 06 톱, 톱질하다 07 바느질하다, 꿰매다 08 (씨를) 뿌리다, 심다 09 환대, 접대 10 적대감

C 01 ethical 02 consistent 03 precedes 04 addiction 05 substitute 06 in

DAY 30

A 01 ① 내용(물) ② 목차 ③ 만족하는, 만족시키다 ④ 함(유)량 02 block 03 ① 문제, 쟁점 ② 발행, 호, (책 등을) 출판하다, 발행하다 ③ 발급하다 ④ 나오다 04 even 05 ① 덮다, 가리다 ② 담당하다, 다루다 ③ 보도하다, 취재하다 ④ 표지 06 ① 평평한 ② 납작한 ③ 바람이 빠진, 펑크 난 ④ 아파트 (英) 07 ① 이유, 변명 ② 이성 ③ 추론하다, 생각하다 08 release 09 ① 차이 ② 수익 ③ 가장자리 10 board 11 address 12 ① 봄 ② 샘 ③ 용수철, (갑자기) 튀다[뛰다]

B 01 단계, 국면 02 어구, 구 03 고도, 높이 04 적성, 소질, 경향 05 태도 06 영향을 미치다 07 효과, 영향, 결과 08 도덕의, 도덕적인 09 사기, 의욕 10 죽을 운명인, 치명적인

C 01 interrupted 02 mediate 03 comparative 04 adapt 05 excess 06 flight

FINAL CHECK-UP

DAY 01~03

01 완료하다, 완전한 02 거리, 간격 03 기간, 시기, 시대 04 수입, 소득 05 순간, 중요성 06 믿을 수 있는, 의지가 되는 07 조사하다, 연구하다 08 재료, 자료, 물질, 물질의, 육체적인 09 희미해지다, 사라지다 10 세부 사항, 상세 11 개선하다, 향상하다 12 나누다, 공유하다, 몫 13 특성, 특색 14 낙담시키다, 방해하다 15 바치다, 헌신하다 16 증가하다, 증가시키다, 증가, 인상 17 아주 중요한, 필수적인, 생명 유지에 필요한 18 (대단히) 놀라게 하다 19 분리하다, 별개의, 각각의 20 개정하다, 정정하다 21 믿음, 신념, 신앙 22 결합시키다, 겸비하다 23 목표, 목적, 목표로 하다, 겨냥하다 24 확실한, 확신하는, 어떤 25 손상, 피해, 손상을 입히다 26 범죄, 범행, 죄악 27 양, 수량 28 상황, 위치 29 만기가 된, ~을 하기로 되어 있는 30 성공, 성공작 31 설립하다, 기초를 세우다 32 나타나다, 모습을 드러내다, (생각·사실 등이) 드러나다 33 이루다, 성취하다 34 실용적인, 실제적인 35 거절하다, 거부하다 36 표현하다, 나타내다, 속달로 보내다, 급행의, 신속한, 급행, 속달 37 받아들이다, 수락하다 38 노출시키다, 폭로하다 39 해결, 결심, 결의 40 이루다, 성취하다

DAY 04~06

01 유아, 젖먹이, 아기 02 영향, 충격, 영향[충격]을 주다 03 범주, 부문 04 노력, 수고, 결과 05 발전, 성장, 개발 06 관점, 시각, 원근법 07 토론하다, 논의하다 08 예측하다, 예보하다, 예측, 예보 09 진전, 진보, 진보[발전]하다, 전진하다 10 시도, 재판 11 중요한, 의미 있는, 상당한 12 A에게 B를 제공하다 13 보상, 사례금, 보상하다 14 규칙적인, 정기적인, 보통의, 단골손님 15 복지, 행복 16 고대의, 옛날의 17 ~에 유의하다, ~에 주목하다 18 다루다, 처리하다, 손잡이 19 결정하다, 밝혀내다 20 효율적인, 유능한 21 참가, 참여 22 실망시키다, 낙담시키다 23 의견, 견해 24 혼동하다, 혼란시키다 25 현실적인, 사실주의의 26 ~을 인식하다, ~을 알다, ~을 깨닫다 27 두다, ~의 위치를 알아내다 28 관찰하다, 목격하다, 준수하다 29 모이다, 모으다 30 군대, 군대의 31 금지하다 32 전시하다, 보이다, 전시품 33 존재하다, (근근이) 살아가다 34 발명, 발명품, 날조 35 경보, 불안, 불안하게 하다, 경보를 발하다 36 적절한, 올바른 37 ~을 제외하고, 제외하다 38 배출, 방출, 배출물 39 ~을 떠맡다, ~을 고용하다, (특정한 특질을) 띠다 40 보수적인, 보수주의의

DAY 07~09

01 건설하다, 구성하다 02 문서, 서류, 기록하다 03 정확한, 정밀한, 꼼꼼한 04 옮기다, 갈아타다, 이동, 이전, 환승 05 등록하다, 기록하다, 등록 06 붙잡다, 움켜잡다, 움켜잡음 07 논평, 언급, 의견, 논평하다, 의견을 말하다 08 지속 가능한, 견딜 수 있는 09 지원, 신청(서), 적용 10 버리다, 포기하다 11 정의하다, 규정하다 12 추정하다, 평가하다, 추정, 견적 13 빛나다, 타다, 상기되다, 불빛, 홍조 14 공격적인, 매우 적극적인, 침략적인 15 겉모습, 외모, 출현 16 대안, 양자택일, 대체의, 양자택일의 17 단단한, 확고한, 회사, 단단하게 하다 18 평판, 명성 19 보증하다, 보증, 담보 20 훌륭한, 뛰어난, 눈부신 21 속하다, 제자리에 있다 22 성(性), 성별 23 수술, 운영, 작업 24 편안함, 위로, 편하게 하다, 위로하다 25 행동, 태도 26 투자하다, (시간·노력 등을) 쏟다 27 (대)다수, 대부분 28 정반대의, 맞은편의, 정반대의 것 29 A에게 B를 상기시키다[생각나게 하다] 30 분석하다 31 선언하다, 발표하다, (과세품을) 신고하다 32 거대한, 방대한 33 장벽, 장애물, 한계 34 밀다, 찌르다, 끼어들다, 밀기, 추진력 35 교육, 훈련 36 폭력적인, 격렬한, 심한 37 무죄인, 악의 없는, 순수한 38 제출하다, 굴복하다 39 믿을 수 없는, 놀라운, 대단한 40 할당하다, 임명하다, 지정하다

DAY 10~12

01 상담하다, 상의하다, 참고하다 02 닮다, 유사하다 03 섬세한, 연약한, 정교한 04 역경, 불운 05 일시적인, 임시의 06 생물학의, 생(물)체의 07 떨다, 흔들리다, 걱정하다, 떨림 08 제한하다, 한정하다 09 맞서다, 직면하게 만들다 10 수직의, 세로의 11 밝히다, 폭로하다, 드러내다 12 ~하는 데 어려움을 겪다 13 이행하다, 실행하다, 도구 14 ~와 관계가 있다, ~와 연관되다 15 논리적인, 타당한 16 탄소 17 자산, 재산 18 철사, 전선, (전선을) 연결하다 19 원시의, 원시적인 20 처음의, 초기의, 머리글자 21 분명한, 명백한, 솔직한 22 선거, 당선 23 대화, 대담 24 수평(선)의, 가로의 25 거주하다, 살다 26 동일한, 일치하는 27 양육하다, 육성하다, 촉진하다 28 청소년기 29 파괴적인 30 구조하다, 구조, 구출 31 협상[교섭]하다, 타결하다 32 퇴직하다, 철수하다 33 가난, 빈곤 34 희생, 제물, 희생하다, 제물로 바치다 35 분명한, 외관상의 36 길이, 시간 37 우세한, 지배적인 38 주목할 만한, 놀랄 만한, 훌륭한 39 상호 간의, 서로의, 공동[공통]의 40 위계, 계급(제), 지배층

DAY 13~15

01 종업원, 수행원 02 짜증나게[화나게] 하다, 거슬리다 03 박탈하다, 빼앗다 04 외교관 05 도시의 06 투옥하다, 감금하다 07 관대한, 후한 08 기어가다, 서행하다, 기어가기, 서행 09 정당화하다 10 모험 11 국내의, 가정의 12 주저하다, 망설이다 13 감정을 상하게 하다 14 의심하다, 용의자 15 바꾸다, 이동하다, 변화, 이동, 교대 16 배포하다, 분배하다 17 피난, 은신처, 위안 18 거주자, 레지던트(수련의), 거주하는 19 결과, 성과 20 거만한, 오만한 21 전략 22 절차, 수순 23 특권, 특혜, 특권을 주다 24 기적 25 충실한 26 후보자 27 촉진하다, 홍보하다, 승진시키다 28 지배하다, 우세하다 29 창피를 주다, 굴욕감을 느끼게 하다 30 절망, 절망하다 31 영토, 세력권 32 민주주의, 민주국가 33 참다, 견디다, 용인하다 34 피난처, 주거지, 보호소, 보호하다, 피하다 35 서투른, 어색한 36 열망하는, 열심인 37 진짜의, 진실한 38 (단체의) 장(長), 우두머리, 주요한, 최고의 39 ~에 뒤처지지 않다, ~을 따라가다 40 목적지, 도착지, 목표

DAY 16~18

01 대조, 대비, 대조를 이루다 02 이주하다, (새·동물이) 이동하다 03 번쩍이다, 번쩍임, 플래시 04 혼합, 혼합물 05 마법의 06 역설적으로 07 ~에서 유래하다, ~에서 파생되다 08 정복하다, 극복하다, 이기다 09 걸작, 명작 10 중력, 중대성 11 심오한, 깊은 12 성분, 구성 요소, 부품, 구성하는 13 신경 14 나뭇가지, 지점, 분과 15 조정하다, 동등한 16 소설, 허구 17 연속, 시리즈 18 추상적인, 개요, 추출하다, 요약하다 19 무너지다, 붕괴하다 20 의식, 의식의, 의례적인 21 조직, 화장지 22 종(種), 종류 23 오케스트라, 관현악단 24 인상적인, 감동적인 25 비유, 은유 26 ~을 고려[참작]하다 27 해골, 뼈대 28 귀족의, 고귀한, 귀족 29 물질, 실체, 본질 30 고체, 고체의, 견고한 31 ~을 생각해 내다 32 윤곽을 그리다, 개요를 말하다, 개요, 윤곽 33 (우연히) 만나다, 마주치다, 마주침 34 얕은, 피상적인, 천박한 35 오르다, 올라가다 36 궁극적인, 최고의, 최후의 37 포유동물 38 인류, 인간성, 인간애 39 식민지의 40 건축가

FINAL CHECK-UP

DAY 19~21

01 전형적인, 보통의 02 설치하다, 설비하다 03 작동시키다, 활성화시키다 04 피를 흘리다, 출혈하다 05 괴롭히다, 성가시게 하다, 성가심 06 가르치다, 지시하다 07 ~에서 기인하다, ~에서 비롯되다 08 만성적인, 장기간의 09 섬유, 섬유질 10 설명, 해명 11 전자의 12 존경하다, 감탄하다 13 증상, 징후 14 학생, 눈동자 15 진단하다 16 치료하다, 고치다, 치유(법) 17 타격, 뇌졸중 18 거친, 대강의 19 회로, 순환 20 자발적인, 자원봉사의 21 고립시키다, 격리하다 22 수송하다, 운반하다, 수송 23 통근하다, 통근, 통근 거리[시간] 24 최대화하다 25 신체의, 물질[물리]적인 26 돕다, 조력 27 침략하다, 침입하다 28 ~에 영향을 미치다 29 조리법, 비법, 비결 30 가속하다, 촉진하다 31 여분의, 예비의, 할애하다, 아끼다 32 피할 수 없는, 당연한 33 먹을 수 있는, 식용의 34 면역성의 35 다수의, 수많은 36 집단의, 공동의, 집단 37 (세밀히) 조사하다 38 자세, 자세를 취하다 39 학업의, 학구적인 40 지적인, 지성의, 지식인

DAY 22~24

01 보존[보호]하다, 아끼다 02 낭비하는, 헛된 03 감소하다, 약화시키다 04 깜짝 놀란, 겁먹은 05 열대 우림 06 전환하다, 바꾸다 07 ~을 버리다, ~을 처리하다[없애다] 08 가정, 추측, 인수 09 산(酸), 산성의 10 직물, 천, (사회·건물 등의) 구조 11 ~의 탓[덕분]으로 돌리다, 속성, 자질 12 간섭하다, 방해하다 13 광고, 상업의 14 타고난, 선천적인, 고유의 15 적절한, 적합한 16 불안, 걱정, 염려 17 깨끗이 하다, 정화하다 18 표면, 외관, 수면으로 올라오다, (갑자기) 드러나다 19 변형시키다, 바꾸다 20 낙관적인, 낙관하는 21 응답자 22 멸종 위기에 처한, 위험에 빠진 23 절박한, 필사적인, 자포자기한 24 남아 있다, 여전히 ~인 채로 있다 25 쓸다, 휩쓸다, 쓸기 26 부서지기 쉬운, 취약한 27 집중을 방해하는 것, 주의 산만 28 호기심 29 결국 ~이 되다, 결국 ~하다 30 소중히 하다 31 분명한, 눈에 띄는 32 정보를 주는, 유익한 33 갑작스러운 34 오염 35 시청자, 관객 36 안정된, 견고한 37 말의, 언어의, 구두의 38 칼럼, 기둥 39 보내다, 전송하다, 전염시키다 40 필터, 여과 장치, 여과하다, 거르다

DAY 25~27

01 헛된, 허영심이 많은 02 잇따른, 연속하는 03 원칙, 원리, 신념 04 현상 05 극심한, 치열한 06 (이리저리) 돌아다니다, 배회하다 07 충분한 08 곡선, 커브 09 교장, 우두머리, 주요한, 중요한 10 결함, 결점 11 불길, 불꽃 12 토착의, 원산의, 원주민 13 지진 14 선택적인 15 유래하다, 발생하다, 고안하다 16 열대의, 열대 지방의 17 각각의 18 척박한, 결실이 없는 19 문학의, 문학적인 20 상당한, 꽤 많은 21 중지하다, 취소하다 22 멸종한, 사라진 23 뼈대, 틀, 액자 24 문자 그대로의, 문자(상)의 25 모방하다, 흉내 내다 26 엉망, 혼란한 상태, 더럽히다 27 칭찬, 칭찬하다 28 터무니없는, 불합리한 29 맞는, 올바른, 정정하다, 바로잡다 30 최적의, 최상의 31 뜨다, 떠다니다 32 유행 33 농업 34 얼다, 동결시키다 35 폭발, 분화 36 본능 37 무서워하는 38 기업, 회사, 법인, 조합 39 여성의, 여성스러운 40 (자격·별칭) ~으로 알려져 있다

DAY 28~30

01 감소하다, 하락하다, 감소, 하락, 거절하다, 아래로 경사지다, 아래를 향하다 02 사기, 의욕 03 탐험하다 04 비상사태 05 아주 멋진, 훌륭한 06 효과, 영향, 결과 07 방해하다, 중단하다 08 비교를 통한, 비교의, 상대적인 09 놀람, 두려움 10 ~에 앞서다[선행하다] 11 명상하다, 묵상하다 12 ~을 염려하다, ~을 걱정하다 13 조각상 14 적대감 15 중독, 열중 16 민족의, 종족의 17 순환하다 18 양심 19 개인적인 20 도덕의, 도덕적인 21 지위, 신분, 상황 22 방어[수비]하다, 변호하다 23 불변의, 끊임없는 24 채택하다, 입양하다 25 고도, 높이 26 인원, 직원, 인사과 27 끔찍한, 심한, 지독한 28 혁명, 회전 29 죽을 운명인, 치명적인 30 모의 실험하다 31 ~에 종사하고 있다, ~에 열중하다 32 확인하다, 승인하다, (사실임을) 입증하다 33 계산하다 34 동시에 35 의회, 회의 36 신경 (계통)의 37 ~을 보충하다, ~을 보상하다 38 조언, 상담, 조언하다, 상담하다 39 석방하다, 놓아주다, 석방, 해방 40 수치, 모습, 몸매, 인물, 사람, 모양, 무늬, 이해하다, 생각해 내다

MEMO

MEMO

MEMO

MEMO

MEMO